Functional Programming with Haskell:

Building Reliable, Scalable, and Elegant Software with Pure Functions and Advanced Type Systems"

Matthew D.Passmore

Table of Content

PART I: INTRODUCTION TO FUNCTIONAL PROGRAMMING AND HASKELL

CHAPTER 1

Introduction to Functional Programming

Functional programming is a paradigm of software development centered on functions as the primary building blocks of computation. Unlike imperative programming, which emphasizes changes in state and the execution of sequences of instructions, functional programming focuses on declarative expressions and immutable data.

At its core, functional programming seeks to write code that is clear, concise, and predictable. Key principles include:

Pure Functions: Functions that always produce the same output for a given input without causing side effects (such as modifying external states).

Immutability: Data structures cannot be altered after creation, leading to safer and more predictable programs.

Higher-Order Functions: Functions that can take other functions as inputs or return them as outputs, enabling abstraction and reusability.

Function Composition: Combining simple functions to build complex ones, mirroring the way mathematical functions work.

Lazy Evaluation: Delaying computation until the result is actually needed, optimizing performance.

Functional programming offers several benefits, such as easier debugging, better concurrency handling, and fewer bugs due to its declarative nature and immutability. Popular functional programming languages include Haskell, Scala, Elixir, and Clojure, though many modern languages like Python and JavaScript have adopted functional programming features.

Haskell, in particular, stands out as a purely functional language with a strong type system, making it an excellent choice for learning and mastering functional programming concepts.

What is Functional Programming?

Functional programming (FP) is a programming paradigm that treats computation as the evaluation of mathematical functions and emphasizes a declarative approach to problem-solving. It is based on key principles such as immutability, pure functions, and higher-order functions, aiming to produce more predictable, concise, and reliable code.

Core Concepts of Functional Programming:

Pure Functions

A pure function always produces the same output for the same input and has no side effects (it does not alter global states or interact with external systems).

Example:

haskell
Copy code
```
square x = x * x
```

Immutability

Data cannot be modified after it is created. Instead, new data structures are generated when changes are required. This ensures safer and more predictable operations.

Declarative Style

Instead of specifying "how" to do something, FP focuses on "what" needs to be done, often resembling mathematical expressions.

Higher-Order Functions

Functions can take other functions as arguments or return functions as results, enabling abstraction and modularity.

Function Composition

Small, reusable functions can be combined to form more complex operations, promoting code reusability and clarity.

Lazy Evaluation

Expressions are not evaluated until their results are needed, optimizing performance and allowing infinite data structures.

Advantages of Functional Programming:

Ease of Debugging: Pure functions are predictable and easier to test.
Concurrency-Friendly: Immutability and statelessness make it easier to write concurrent and parallel programs.

Modular Code: Higher-order functions and composition encourage reusable and maintainable code.

Functional programming is widely used in fields like data processing, web development, financial modeling, and machine learning, and it has influenced modern languages like Python, JavaScript, and Kotlin. Haskell, a purely functional language, remains one of the most powerful tools for mastering FP concepts.

Key Concepts of Functional Programming

Functional programming revolves around several foundational concepts that distinguish it from other programming paradigms. These principles promote clean, reliable, and maintainable code by focusing on functions and immutability.

1. Pure Functions

A pure function produces the same output for the same input without causing side effects. It doesn't modify external states or rely on them. This predictability makes code easier to test and debug.

Example in Haskell:

haskell
Copy code
```
add x y = x + y
```

2. Immutability

Data in functional programming is immutable, meaning once created, it cannot be changed. Instead of modifying existing data, new data structures are created, ensuring safety and predictability.

3. First-Class and Higher-Order Functions

Functions are treated as first-class citizens, meaning they can be assigned to variables, passed as arguments, and returned from other functions.

A higher-order function takes other functions as inputs or returns functions.

Example in Haskell:
haskell
Copy code
```
applyTwice f x = f (f x)
```

4. Function Composition

Smaller functions can be combined to create more complex operations. This promotes reusability and modularity in code.
Example in Haskell:

haskell
Copy code

compose f g x = f (g x)

5. Declarative Programming

Functional programming focuses on what needs to be done rather than how it is done, emphasizing clear and concise logic over step-by-step instructions.

6. Recursion

In functional programming, loops are typically replaced by recursion, where a function calls itself to solve smaller instances of a problem.

7. Lazy Evaluation

Expressions are evaluated only when their results are required, optimizing performance and enabling infinite data structures like streams.

8. Algebraic Data Types and Pattern Matching

Haskell's algebraic data types allow the creation of complex data structures, while pattern matching simplifies their manipulation.

9. Monads and Effects

Monads provide a way to handle side effects, such as IO or state changes, while keeping the core logic pure. This enables functional programming to interact with the real world while maintaining immutability and purity.

Summary

These concepts work together to create a programming paradigm that emphasizes clarity, safety, and scalability. Functional programming is particularly valuable for writing concurrent applications, data transformations, and highly abstract, reusable solutions. Haskell serves as a prime example of a language that embodies these principles.

The Benefits of Functional Programming

Functional programming (FP) offers numerous advantages that make it a powerful paradigm for building robust, maintainable, and efficient software. By focusing on immutability, pure functions, and declarative logic, FP addresses many challenges faced in traditional programming.

1. Improved Code Reliability and Predictability

Pure Functions: Since pure functions always produce the same output for the same input, they are predictable and easier to debug.
Immutability: By avoiding changes to data, FP eliminates issues related to mutable state, reducing bugs caused by unintended side effects.

2. Enhanced Modularity and Reusability

Higher-Order Functions: Functions that take other functions as arguments or return functions enable the creation of reusable, composable code.
Function Composition: Small, independent functions can be combined to form complex operations, improving code clarity and reusability.

3. Ease of Testing and Debugging

Pure functions and immutability simplify testing since there is no need to account for side effects or shared state.
Functional programs are easier to reason about because each function operates in isolation from others.

4. Concurrency and Parallelism

.FP is inherently thread-safe because of immutability, making it ideal for concurrent and parallel programming.

Stateless computations allow tasks to run independently, improving performance on multi-core processors.

5. Declarative and Concise Code

FP emphasizes what needs to be done, not how, leading to shorter and more readable code.
Abstractions like map, filter, and reduce enable complex data transformations with minimal code.

6. Lazy Evaluation and Performance Optimization

Expressions in FP are evaluated only when their results are needed, reducing unnecessary computations and enabling the handling of large or infinite data structures.

7. Mathematical Elegance and Formal Reasoning

FP is closely aligned with mathematical principles, enabling developers to formally reason about program behavior. This reduces the likelihood of logical errors.

8. Scalability for Complex Systems

Functional programming's modularity and composability allow for the development of scalable, maintainable systems that grow in complexity without becoming unmanageable.

9. Cross-Disciplinary Applications

FP is widely used in areas like data science, machine learning, and finance, where transformations and immutability are critical.
Languages like Haskell, Scala, and Python leverage FP principles to build high-performance applications.

Conclusion

Functional programming offers a cleaner, safer, and more efficient approach to software development. Its focus on immutability, pure functions, and declarative logic makes it a valuable paradigm for modern applications, particularly in environments requiring high reliability, concurrency, and scalability.

Functional Programming vs. Imperative Programming

Functional programming (FP) and imperative programming (IP) represent two distinct paradigms for writing software. While both aim to solve computational problems, they differ significantly in their approach, focus, and implementation.

1. Approach to Problem-Solving

Functional Programming:

Focuses on what needs to be done.
Uses declarative statements to describe desired outcomes.
Example: Transforming a list with map or filter.

Imperative Programming:

Focuses on how to achieve a result.
Involves step-by-step instructions that manipulate state.
Example: Using for loops to iterate through a list.

2. State and Mutability

Functional Programming:

Relies on immutability. Data structures cannot be changed after creation.
Avoids shared state, reducing potential side effects and bugs.

Imperative Programming:

Relies on mutable state. Variables can be updated as the program executes.
Changes to shared state can lead to unintended consequences and harder-to-debug code.

3. Functions vs. Procedures

Functional Programming:

Treats functions as first-class citizens (they can be passed as arguments, returned, or assigned).
Focuses on pure functions—functions with no side effects.

Imperative Programming:

Emphasizes procedures or routines, which may manipulate state or have side effects.
Functions often depend on or modify external states.

4. Concurrency and Parallelism

Functional Programming:

Thread-safe by default due to immutability.
Easier to write concurrent and parallel programs.

Imperative Programming:

Requires careful handling of shared state in multithreading, increasing complexity.
Prone to race conditions and deadlocks without proper synchronization.

5. Code Style

Functional Programming:

Declarative and concise. Operations like map, reduce, and filter simplify code.
Promotes modularity by composing smaller functions.

Imperative Programming:

Verbose and explicit. Requires detailed instructions for each operation.
Often involves loops, conditional statements, and iterative processes.

6. Examples in Practice

Functional Style Example (Haskell):

haskell
Copy code
```haskell
squaredNumbers = map (\x -> x * x) [1, 2, 3, 4, 5]
```
Imperative Style Example (Python):

python
Copy code
```python
squared_numbers = []
for x in [1, 2, 3, 4, 5]:
    squared_numbers.append(x * x)
```

7. Use Cases

Functional Programming:

Ideal for data transformation, parallel processing, and systems requiring high reliability.
Common in fields like data science, finance, and machine learning.

Imperative Programming:

Suited for scenarios requiring fine-grained control of hardware or sequential tasks.
Common in game development, system programming, and embedded systems.

Conclusion

While functional programming emphasizes immutability, declarative logic, and purity, imperative programming focuses on mutable state and step-by-step instructions. Each paradigm has its strengths and is suited to different problem domains, but FP's modularity and safety make it increasingly popular in modern software development.

CHAPTER 2

Getting Started with Haskell

Haskell is a purely functional programming language known for its expressive syntax, strong type system, and lazy evaluation. It is designed to promote concise, reliable, and maintainable code, making it ideal for both academic and industrial applications.

Key Features of Haskell:

Purely Functional: Haskell enforces pure functions, making your programs predictable and easier to debug.

Strong, Static Typing: The type system ensures errors are caught at compile time, improving code safety.

Lazy Evaluation: Computations are deferred until their results are needed, optimizing performance and enabling infinite data structures.

Immutability: Once defined, data cannot be changed, leading to more robust and thread-safe applications.

Setting Up Haskell Development Environment

To start programming in Haskell, you need to set up a development environment that includes the necessary tools for writing, compiling, and running Haskell programs. The following steps guide you through the installation and configuration process.

1. Install Haskell Platform (or GHCup)

The Glasgow Haskell Compiler (GHC) is the primary compiler for Haskell. You can install it via GHCup, a tool that simplifies the management of Haskell tools, including GHC, Cabal, and Stack.

GHCup Installation:

GHCup is the recommended way to install Haskell-related tools. It ensures that you have the latest versions of GHC, Cabal, and Stack.

Visit the official GHCup website and follow the installation instructions for your operating system (Windows, macOS, Linux).
Run the following command in your terminal (Linux/macOS) or Command Prompt (Windows):
bash
Copy code

```
curl --proto '=https' --tlsv1.2 -sSf https://get-ghcup.haskell.org | sh
```

After installation, you can check the versions of installed tools:

bash
Copy code
```
ghc --version
cabal --version
stack --version
```

2. Install a Text Editor or IDE

While you can write Haskell code in any text editor, a good editor or IDE with syntax highlighting, autocompletion, and other features makes development easier.

Visual Studio Code (VSCode):

Install Visual Studio Code.
Install the Haskell extension from the marketplace: Haskell Language Server.
This provides features like syntax highlighting, linting, and debugging for Haskell.

Vim/Emacs:

For those familiar with terminal editors, both Vim and Emacs offer Haskell syntax support and plugins, like haskell-vim-now or haskell-mode for Emacs.

IntelliJ IDEA:
If you prefer IntelliJ IDEA, you can use the Haskell plugin for development.

3. Install Cabal and Stack

Cabal and Stack are Haskell build tools. Both are used for managing packages, dependencies, and building Haskell projects, but Stack provides additional features such as managing GHC versions per project.

Cabal:

Cabal is a build tool and package manager. It is part of the Haskell Platform and can be installed via GHCup.
To initialize a new project, you can run:

bash
Copy code
cabal init

Stack:

Stack simplifies the process of managing dependencies and building Haskell projects.

It ensures reproducible builds and supports various GHC versions.

To install Stack via GHCup, run:

bash
Copy code
ghcup install stack

After installation, you can create a new project:

bash
Copy code
stack new my-project

cd my-project

stack setup

stack build

stack exec

4. Verify the Setup

Once GHC, Cabal, Stack, and your editor are installed, you can verify your environment by running a simple "Hello, World!" program.

Create a file called hello.hs:

haskell

Copy code

```
main :: IO ()
main = putStrLn "Hello, Haskell!"
```

Compile and run it:

bash

Copy code

```
ghc hello.hs
./hello
```

If everything is set up correctly, you should see the output "Hello, Haskell!" in your terminal.

5. Optional Tools

GHCi:

GHCi is the interactive shell for GHC. It allows you to quickly test Haskell expressions without needing to compile a full program. Simply type ghci in the terminal to enter the interactive mode.

HLint:
HLint is a tool that provides suggestions to improve your Haskell code. It is widely used to enforce good coding practices.

Conclusion

By following these steps, you'll have a complete Haskell development environment set up, ready for creating and running Haskell programs. Whether you prefer using

GHCup with Stack for version management or Cabal for simple project builds, Haskell provides a robust platform for functional programming.

First Steps in Haskell: Hello World

Getting started with Haskell begins with writing the classic "Hello, World!" program. This simple program demonstrates Haskell's basic syntax and the process of running a functional program.

Step 1: Create the Program

Open your text editor or Integrated Development Environment (IDE).

Create a new file called hello.hs.

Write the following code:

haskell

Copy code

```haskell
main :: IO ()
main = putStrLn "Hello, World!"
```

Explanation:

main: The entry point of any Haskell program.
:: IO (): Indicates that the main function performs input/output (IO) operations and returns no meaningful value (() is the unit type).
putStrLn: A function to print a string followed by a newline to the console.

Step 2: Compile the Program

Open your terminal or command prompt.

Navigate to the directory containing hello.hs.

Compile the program using the Glasgow Haskell Compiler (GHC):

bash
Copy code
ghc hello.hs

This will generate an executable file called hello (or hello.exe on Windows).

Step 3: Run the Program

Run the compiled program:

bash
Copy code
./hello
You should see the output:

Copy code
Hello, World!

Running the Program with GHCi

For quick testing, you can use GHC's interactive shell (GHCi) instead of

compiling the program:

Start GHCi by typing ghci in your terminal.

Load the hello.hs file:

haskell

Copy code

:load hello

Run the main function:

haskell

Copy code

main

You will see the output directly in the terminal.

Understanding the Program

Purity in Haskell: Haskell separates pure functions from functions that involve side effects like printing to the console. The IO type in the main function signals the use of side effects.
Minimal Syntax: Haskell's syntax is concise, focusing on readability and simplicity.

Conclusion

Writing the "Hello, World!" program in Haskell is a straightforward way to explore its structure and execution model. By understanding the main function and basic IO, you've taken your first step toward functional programming with Haskell.

Exploring Haskell Syntax and Structure

Haskell is a statically-typed, functional programming language with a strong emphasis on immutability, pure functions, and a rich type system. To get started, it's essential to understand the basic syntax and structure that make Haskell unique. Below, we will explore Haskell's key syntax features and program structure.

1. Basic Program Structure

A simple Haskell program typically consists of:

Imports: Bringing in libraries or modules that provide additional functionality.
Main Function: The entry point for the program, typically where IO actions occur.

Example:

haskell
Copy code
```
module Main where

main :: IO ()
main = putStrLn "Hello, Haskell!"
```
module Main where declares the module name.
main :: IO () defines the main function with the IO action.

putStrLn "Hello, Haskell!" is the action that prints the string to the console.

2. Functions

Functions in Haskell are defined using the functionName parameter = expression syntax. Haskell functions are curried by default, meaning they take one argument at a time.

Example:

haskell
Copy code
```
add :: Int -> Int -> Int
add x y = x + y
```
add :: Int -> Int -> Int is the function's type signature. It means add takes two integers and returns an integer.
add x y = x + y defines the function add, which adds two numbers.

3. Types and Type Signatures

Haskell has a strong, static type system, meaning that the types of values are known at compile time.

Type Signatures: Optional but encouraged, they describe the types of functions.

Example:

haskell
Copy code
```
multiply :: Int -> Int -> Int
multiply x y = x * y
```

Int -> Int -> Int is the type signature, indicating that multiply takes two Int values and returns an Int.
Haskell includes many built-in types, such as Int, Double, Bool, and String, along with more advanced types like lists, tuples, and algebraic data types (ADTs).

4. Lists

Lists are fundamental in Haskell and are denoted by square brackets []. Lists can hold any type of elements, and elements of the same type must be homogeneous.

Example:

haskell
Copy code
```
numbers :: [Int]
numbers = [1, 2, 3, 4, 5]
```
numbers is a list of integers [1, 2, 3, 4, 5].

Lists in Haskell are immutable by default, meaning once created, they cannot be altered. You can manipulate them using higher-order functions like map, filter, and foldr.

5. Tuples

A tuple is an ordered collection of elements of potentially different types. They are defined using parentheses ().

Example:

haskell
Copy code
```
coordinates :: (Int, Int)
coordinates = (10, 20)
```

coordinates is a tuple containing two Int values, (10, 20). Tuples are useful for grouping related data without the overhead of creating a custom data type.

6. Conditionals

Haskell uses guards and if-then-else constructs for conditional logic.

if-then-else:
Example:

haskell
Copy code
```
isEven :: Int -> Bool
isEven x = if x `mod` 2 == 0 then True else False
```

Guards:

Guards provide more flexibility than if-then-else and are typically used in function definitions.

Example:

haskell
Copy code
```
absolute :: Int -> Int
absolute x
  | x >= 0    = x
  | otherwise = -x
```

Here, the function checks the value of x and applies different expressions based on conditions.

7. Pattern Matching

Pattern matching is a way to handle different cases in a function definition. It's used for deconstructing data types and checking for specific values.

Example (for lists):

haskell
Copy code
```
head' :: [a] -> a
head' [] = error "Empty list"
head' (x:_) = x
```
head' [] = error "Empty list" handles the case of an empty list.

head' (x:_) = x handles the case where the list has at least one element. The _ means we don't care about the rest of the list.
Pattern matching is a powerful feature that allows for concise and readable code.

8. Let and Where

Let: Defines local variables within an expression. It's often used inside expressions like do blocks or lambda functions.

Example:

haskell
Copy code
```
let x = 3 in x + 5
```

Where: Defines local variables at the end of a function definition, providing cleaner syntax for more complex expressions.

Example:

haskell
Copy code
```
area :: Float -> Float -> Float
area width height = width * height
  where width = 5
        height = 10
```

9. Lambdas

Lambdas (or anonymous functions) allow you to define functions without naming them. They're used for short functions that are passed as arguments to higher-order functions.

Example:

haskell

Copy code

```
addOne :: Int -> Int
addOne = \x -> x + 1
```

\x -> x + 1 is a lambda function that takes x and returns x + 1.

10. IO Actions

Haskell distinguishes between pure functions (which have no side effects) and impure functions (which involve side effects, like IO operations). IO actions are represented by the IO type.

Example:

haskell
Copy code
```
main :: IO ()
main = do
  putStrLn "What is your name?"
  name <- getLine
  putStrLn ("Hello, " ++ name)
```

putStrLn and getLine are IO functions.
The <- operator is used to extract values from IO actions.

Conclusion

Haskell's syntax is minimalistic but expressive. Key concepts such as functions, types, pattern matching, and immutability form the foundation of Haskell programming. As you grow familiar with these basic structures, you'll be able to explore Haskell's more advanced features like type classes, monads, and concurrency, which make it a powerful language for functional programming.

PART II: PURE FUNCTIONS AND IMMUTABILITY

CHAPTER 3
Pure Functions in Depth

Pure functions are the cornerstone of functional programming. They adhere to two fundamental principles:

Deterministic Behavior: A pure function always produces the same output for the same input, irrespective of external factors.

No Side Effects: Pure functions do not alter state, interact with external systems, or perform actions like modifying variables, printing to a console, or accessing databases.

Characteristics of Pure Functions

Referential Transparency: A pure function can be replaced with its output value without changing the program's behavior.

Immutability: Pure functions do not modify their arguments or any external state.

Example of a Pure Function

haskell

Copy code

```
square :: Int -> Int
square x = x * x
```

Deterministic: For every input x, the output is always x * x.

No Side Effects: It only computes the result and does not interact with external systems.

Example of an Impure Function

haskell

Copy code

```
getTime :: IO String
getTime = show <$> getCurrentTime
```

This function is impure because it depends on the system clock, producing a different result every time it is called.

Benefits of Pure Functions

Easier Testing: Since pure functions are deterministic, testing becomes straightforward.
Improved Debugging: With no hidden state changes or side effects, debugging is simplified.
Enhanced Parallelism: Pure functions are inherently thread-safe, making them ideal for concurrent or parallel programming.

Conclusion

Pure functions form the foundation of reliable and maintainable code in Haskell. By adhering to purity,

Haskell programs minimize side effects, making them easier to reason about, test, and optimize.

Definition of Pure Functions

A pure function is a function that exhibits two key characteristics:

Deterministic Output: A pure function always produces the same output for a given set of inputs, regardless of any external factors or system state.
No Side Effects: Pure functions do not alter any external state, interact with external systems, or perform operations such as modifying global variables, printing to the console, or reading from a file.

Formal Definition

In functional programming, a function f is pure if:

f(x) = y for a given x always results in the same y.

Evaluating f(x) has no observable effects other than returning the result y.

Example of a Pure Function

haskell

Copy code

```
add :: Int -> Int -> Int
add x y = x + y
```

Deterministic: For any inputs x and y, the result will always be x + y.

No Side Effects: The function does not depend on or alter any external state.

Example of an Impure Function

haskell

Copy code

```
greet :: String -> IO ()
greet name = putStrLn ("Hello, " ++ name)
```

This function is impure because:

It performs an IO operation (putStrLn) that interacts with the external environment.
The result of calling greet is an observable side effect (printing to the console), not just a return value.

Importance of Pure Functions

Predictability: Pure functions are easier to understand and reason about due to their deterministic nature.
Testability: They are simple to test since the output depends solely on the input.
Composability: Pure functions can be composed together to build more complex logic without introducing unexpected behavior.

By ensuring that functions remain pure, Haskell promotes reliability, maintainability, and clean code design.

Advantages of Pure Functions in Software Development

Pure functions are fundamental to functional programming and offer numerous advantages in software development. These benefits contribute to creating more reliable, maintainable, and efficient codebases.

1. Predictability and Debugging

Pure functions are deterministic, meaning they always produce the same output for the same input. This predictability simplifies debugging, as developers can trace issues by analyzing inputs and outputs without worrying about hidden state changes or external dependencies.

2. Ease of Testing

Testing pure functions is straightforward because they do not rely on external systems or mutable states. Unit tests can focus solely on verifying the function's logic, making tests more robust and less prone to failure due to unrelated factors.

3. Reusability and Modularity

Pure functions are self-contained and independent of external states, making them highly reusable. They can be easily composed and combined to build complex systems without unexpected interactions or side effects.

4. Parallelism and Concurrency

Since pure functions do not modify shared state or depend on external variables, they are inherently thread-safe. This makes it easier to implement parallel or concurrent programming, maximizing performance on multi-core systems.

5. Referential Transparency

Pure functions ensure referential transparency, meaning they can be replaced by their output value without altering the program's behavior. This property facilitates reasoning about the code and allows for compiler optimizations like memoization and lazy evaluation.

6. Immutability and Reliability

Pure functions promote immutability by working with immutable data. This reduces the risk of bugs caused by unintended state changes, resulting in more reliable and maintainable software.

7. Enhanced Maintainability

Code written with pure functions is easier to understand, maintain, and refactor. The absence of side effects and external dependencies simplifies changes and reduces the likelihood of introducing new bugs.

Conclusion

Pure functions bring clarity, reliability, and scalability to software development. By adhering to purity, developers can write code that is easier to test, debug, and maintain, while also unlocking performance benefits through parallelism and optimization. These advantages make pure functions an essential tool for building robust and future-proof software systems.

Referential Transparency

Referential transparency is a fundamental concept in functional programming that describes an expression's behavior when evaluated. An expression is considered referentially transparent if it can be replaced by its resulting value without changing the overall behavior of the program.

Definition

A function or expression is referentially transparent if:

Its evaluation is pure, meaning it does not rely on or alter external states.

It always produces the same output for the same input.

Replacing the function or expression with its value does not affect the correctness of the program.

Example of Referential Transparency
In Haskell:

haskell
Copy code
```haskell
square :: Int -> Int
square x = x * x
```

The function square 4 evaluates to 16.
Replacing square 4 with 16 anywhere in the code will not change the program's behavior.

Example of Lack of Referential Transparency

haskell
Copy code
```haskell
getTime :: IO String
```

```
getTime = show <$> getCurrentTime
```

This function depends on the current system time, which changes continuously.

Calling getTime multiple times may return different results, so it cannot be replaced with a single value.

Benefits of Referential Transparency

Simplifies Reasoning: Code is easier to understand and predict since expressions behave consistently.

Facilitates Debugging: Errors can be traced by examining inputs and outputs without worrying about hidden side effects.

Enables Optimization: The compiler can safely optimize referentially transparent code using techniques like caching or memoization.

Encourages Purity: Promotes the use of pure functions, leading to more reliable and maintainable software.

Conclusion

Referential transparency is a cornerstone of functional programming that ensures code is predictable, testable, and efficient. By adhering to this principle, developers can write cleaner, more robust, and easily optimizable programs.

CHAPTER 4

Immutability and State Management

Immutability is the concept of creating data structures that cannot be altered after their creation. In functional programming, immutability is a core principle that ensures data integrity and simplifies state management by preventing unexpected changes.

Immutability in Functional Programming

No In-Place Modifications: Instead of modifying existing data, new data structures are created with the desired changes.
Predictability: Immutable data ensures consistent behavior, making programs easier to understand and debug.

Example in Haskell:

haskell
Copy code
```
updateList :: [Int] -> [Int]
updateList xs = xs ++ [10]
```

Here, the original list xs remains unchanged, and a new list is created with 10 appended.

Benefits of Immutability in State Management

Easier Reasoning: With no mutable state, developers can focus on data flow without worrying about hidden side effects.

Thread-Safety: Immutable data eliminates race conditions, enabling safer parallel and concurrent programming.
Time-Travel Debugging: Immutable states allow tracking and reverting changes over time, simplifying debugging.

State Management

In functional programming, state is managed through:

Pure Functions: State changes are represented as transformations of immutable data.
Higher-Order Functions: Functions like map, reduce, and fold help manage state transitions declaratively.
Monads: Constructs like the State monad in Haskell allow for explicit and controlled state management without mutability.

Conclusion

Immutability and functional state management reduce complexity, enhance reliability, and make software easier to maintain. These principles are essential for building scalable and robust applications in functional programming languages like Haskell.

The Concept of Immutability

Immutability refers to the property of data that prevents it from being changed after it has been created. Instead of modifying existing data, new copies are created with the desired updates. This concept is fundamental in functional programming and promotes reliability and predictability in software development.

Characteristics of Immutability

No In-Place Changes: Data structures remain unchanged after they are initialized. Any "modifications" result in the creation of a new data structure.

Thread-Safe: Immutable data can be safely shared across threads without risk of race conditions or unintended side effects.

Predictability: Since data doesn't change unexpectedly, programs become easier to understand and debug.

Example of Immutability

In Haskell:

haskell

Copy code

```haskell
addToList :: [Int] -> [Int]
addToList xs = xs ++ [10]
```

The original list xs remains unchanged.
A new list is created with 10 appended, preserving immutability.

Benefits of Immutability

Enhanced Reliability: Prevents bugs caused by unintended changes to shared data.

Simplified Debugging: Immutable data ensures consistent states, making it easier to trace and debug issues.

Ease of Reasoning: Developers can reason about the state of the program without considering external mutations.

Facilitates Parallelism: Immutability enables safe concurrent processing since data cannot be altered by multiple threads.

Immutability in Functional Programming

In functional programming, immutability is tightly integrated with pure functions. These functions operate on immutable data, ensuring no side effects or hidden state changes. Concepts like persistent data structures and monads support immutable workflows.

Conclusion

Immutability ensures consistency, clarity, and safety in software development. By embracing immutability, functional programming languages like Haskell enable developers to write robust, maintainable, and scalable applications.

Managing State in Functional Programming

In functional programming, managing state is a key challenge since the paradigm emphasizes immutability and avoids direct state mutation. Instead of altering shared or global state, functional programming uses declarative and composable techniques to manage state transitions in a predictable and controlled manner.

Key Principles of State Management

Immutability: State is never modified directly. New states are derived from existing ones without altering the original data.
Pure Functions: State transitions are expressed as pure functions, ensuring that state updates are deterministic and side-effect-free.
Explicit State Handling: State changes are explicitly passed through function arguments and return values, avoiding hidden dependencies.

Techniques for State Management

Function Parameters and Return Values

Functions explicitly receive the current state as input and return the new state.

Example in Haskell:

haskell
Copy code
```
updateState :: Int -> Int
updateState x = x + 1
```
This function takes the current state x and returns the updated state without modifying the original.

State Monad

The State monad encapsulates state transformations, providing a clean and composable way to manage state.

Example:

haskell

Copy code

```
import Control.Monad.State

increment :: State Int Int
increment = do
  state <- get
  put (state + 1)
  return state
```

Here, the State monad tracks and updates the state in a controlled manner.

Immutable Data Structures

Persistent data structures are used to represent state changes efficiently without copying entire data sets. Libraries like Data.Map in Haskell provide immutable data structures for managing state.

Functional Lenses

Lenses are used for accessing and updating nested state in an immutable way.

Example with the lens library:

haskell
Copy code
set _1 42 (10, "hello") -- Updates the first element of a tuple

Benefits of Functional State Management

Predictability: State transitions are explicit and deterministic, making programs easier to understand.
Thread Safety: Immutability ensures that concurrent processes can safely work with state.
Modularity: State is localized and managed in small, composable units, enhancing maintainability.
Debugging and Testing: With explicit state handling and pure functions, debugging and testing become simpler.

Conclusion

Managing state in functional programming requires a shift from traditional imperative approaches. By leveraging immutability, pure functions, and advanced techniques like monads and lenses, developers can achieve predictable, scalable, and robust state management, as exemplified in languages like Haskell.

Using Immutable Data Structures in Haskell

In Haskell, immutable data structures are a core concept that aligns with the functional programming paradigm. Immutable data structures cannot be changed after they are created, which promotes safety, simplicity, and predictability in code. Instead of modifying existing data, new structures are created based on the old ones with the desired changes. This approach avoids side effects, ensuring that data remains consistent throughout the program.

Characteristics of Immutable Data Structures

No In-Place Modifications: Once created, data structures cannot be altered. Instead, operations create new versions of the structure.
Efficient Sharing: Immutable structures can share parts of their internal data with previous versions, optimizing memory usage and performance.
Thread-Safety: Since data cannot be mutated, immutable data structures are inherently safe for concurrent and parallel processing.

Types of Immutable Data Structures in Haskell

Lists

Lists in Haskell are naturally immutable. Operations on lists, such as adding or removing elements, return new lists without modifying the original list.

Example:

haskell
Copy code

```
myList = [1, 2, 3]
newList = 0 : myList  -- newList is [0, 1, 2, 3]
```

Tuples

Tuples, like lists, are immutable. You cannot change individual elements of a tuple once it's created.

Example:

haskell
Copy code

```
myTuple = (1, "hello")
newTuple = (2, "world")  -- creates a new tuple
```

Maps (from Data.Map library)

Data.Map provides immutable, efficient key-value mappings. New maps are created when items are added or updated, but the old map remains unchanged.

Example:

haskell
Copy code

```
import qualified Data.Map as Map

myMap = Map.fromList [(1, "one"), (2, "two")]
newMap = Map.insert 3 "three" myMap  -- creates a new
map
```

Sets (from Data.Set library)

Data.Set provides immutable sets that allow for efficient union, intersection, and difference operations. Each operation returns a new set.

Example:

haskell
Copy code

```
import qualified Data.Set as Set

mySet = Set.fromList [1, 2, 3]
```

```
newSet = Set.insert 4 mySet  -- creates a new set
```

Arrays (from Data.Array library)

Haskell also supports immutable arrays. Operations on arrays, such as updates, return new arrays without altering the original.

Example:

haskell
Copy code
```
import Data.Array

myArray = array (1, 3) [(1, "a"), (2, "b"), (3, "c")]
newArray = myArray // [(2, "z")]  -- creates a new array
```

Benefits of Immutable Data Structures

Simplified Reasoning: With immutability, data cannot be unexpectedly changed, which makes it easier to understand the program's flow and reasoning about state changes.

Safer Concurrency: Since immutable structures can't be modified, they are inherently thread-safe, allowing safe parallel processing.

No Side Effects: All changes result in new data structures, eliminating side effects and ensuring that functions behave predictably.

Memory Efficiency: Many immutable data structures are implemented using structural sharing, where unchanged parts of the structure are shared between versions. This makes them more memory-efficient than they might appear at first glance.

Common Operations on Immutable Data Structures

Map: Transforming elements in a collection (e.g., using map on lists).
Fold: Reducing a collection to a single value (e.g., using foldl or foldr).

Insert, Delete, Update: Operations that return new versions of a structure without changing the original.

Example of using map to transform a list:

haskell
Copy code
```
incrementList :: [Int] -> [Int]
incrementList xs = map (+1) xs
```

This creates a new list with each element incremented by 1, leaving the original list unchanged.

Conclusion

Immutable data structures in Haskell offer significant advantages in terms of safety, predictability, and performance. By ensuring that data cannot be modified after creation, Haskell provides a strong foundation for functional programming, where reasoning about code becomes easier, and concurrency becomes safer. Whether using lists, maps, sets, or arrays, Haskell's immutable structures make state management more manageable and error-free.

PART III: ADVANCED TYPES AND TYPE SYSTEM

CHAPTER 5
Haskell's Type System

Haskell's type system is one of its most powerful features, providing a robust framework for creating reliable, bug-free programs. It is strong, static, and inferential, allowing for early error detection, type safety, and expressive type definitions.

Key Features of Haskell's Type System

Static Typing

Types are checked at compile-time, ensuring that errors related to types are caught early before execution.

Example:

haskell

Copy code

```
add :: Int -> Int -> Int  -- Type signature for a function that takes two Ints and returns an Int
add x y = x + y
```

Strong Typing

Haskell's type system enforces strict type checks, meaning that you cannot mix incompatible types without explicit conversion.

Example:

haskell

Copy code

```
"hello" + 5  -- Error, cannot add a string to an integer
```

Type Inference

Haskell automatically infers types, so you don't always have to explicitly specify them. The compiler can determine the correct types based on the code context.

Example:

haskell

Copy code

```
x = 5  -- Haskell infers that x has type Int
```

Polymorphism

Haskell supports parametric polymorphism (generics), where functions can work with any type. This is achieved using type variables.

Example:

haskell

Copy code

```
identity :: a -> a  -- Takes any type and returns the same
type
identity x = x
```

Algebraic Data Types (ADTs)

ADTs allow the creation of custom types by combining other types using sum types (e.g., Either, Maybe) and product types (e.g., Tuples, Records).

Example:

haskell
Copy code
```
data Maybe a = Nothing | Just a  -- A type that represents an optional value
```

Type Classes

Type classes allow you to define generic functions that work for any type that implements the class. They enable polymorphism beyond parametric types.

Example:

haskell
Copy code
```
class Eq a where
  (==) :: a -> a -> Bool  -- Defines equality for a type
```

Benefits of Haskell's Type System

Safety and Reliability: Type errors are caught at compile time, making programs less likely to fail at runtime.
Expressiveness: Haskell's type system allows you to define highly abstract and reusable functions while maintaining strong guarantees.
Concise and Clear Code: Type inference reduces boilerplate, letting you write code that is both compact and easy to understand.
Optimized Performance: With static types, Haskell can optimize programs at compile-time, leading to efficient runtime performance.

Conclusion

Haskell's type system combines the benefits of static typing, strong type checks, and powerful abstractions like polymorphism and type classes to enable the creation of highly reliable, expressive, and efficient programs. Its type system ensures that programs are safe, understandable, and maintainable, making it a cornerstone of Haskell's functional programming approach.

Understanding Types and Type Signatures

In Haskell, types define the kind of values a variable can hold or a function can return. The type system is a foundational element of Haskell's safety and reliability, helping to catch errors at compile time and providing clarity about code behavior. A type signature explicitly describes the types of inputs and outputs for a function, making the code self-documenting and easier to understand.

What Are Types?

A type represents a category of values. For example:

Int represents integers.

Float represents floating-point numbers.
Char represents single characters.
Bool represents boolean values (True or False).
Custom types can also be defined using algebraic data types (ADTs).

What Are Type Signatures?

A type signature explicitly states the types of arguments a function takes and the type it returns. While Haskell can infer types automatically, adding type signatures improves readability and ensures correctness.

Example:
haskell
Copy code
```
add :: Int -> Int -> Int
add x y = x + y
```
Int -> Int -> Int means the function takes two integers as arguments and returns an integer.
The arrow (->) separates argument types and the return type.

Type Signature Syntax

Function Name

Followed by :: (read as "has the type").

Input Types

Each argument's type is listed, separated by ->.

Return Type

The final type after all arrows represents the return value.

Example:

haskell

Copy code

```
greet :: String -> String
greet name = "Hello, " ++ name
```

Polymorphic Types

Haskell supports parametric polymorphism, allowing functions to work with any type.

Example:

haskell

Copy code

```
identity :: a -> a
identity x = x
```

Here, a is a type variable that can represent any type.

Curried Functions

Functions in Haskell are curried, meaning they take arguments one at a time.

Example:

haskell

Copy code

```
multiply :: Int -> Int -> Int
multiply x y = x * y
```

This is equivalent to:

haskell

Copy code

```
multiply :: Int -> (Int -> Int)
```

multiply takes an Int and returns another function that takes an Int and produces an Int.

Benefits of Types and Type Signatures

Error Detection: Types ensure that invalid operations are caught at compile time.
Readability: Type signatures act as documentation for what a function expects and produces.
Reusability: Generic types (e.g., polymorphic functions) allow for reusable and abstract code.
Safety: Types prevent unintended operations, ensuring data consistency.

Conclusion

Understanding types and type signatures is crucial in Haskell, as they form the backbone of its robust and expressive type system. By leveraging types effectively, developers can write safe, maintainable, and easily understandable programs, ensuring both correctness and clarity.

Type Inference in Haskell

Type inference in Haskell refers to the compiler's ability to automatically deduce the types of expressions without explicit type annotations. This powerful feature makes Haskell code more concise while maintaining the benefits of static typing, such as early error detection and type safety.

How Type Inference Works

Haskell uses the Hindley-Milner type inference algorithm to deduce types. The compiler:

Analyzes Expressions: It looks at how functions and variables are used.
Infers Constraints: Determines relationships between types based on usage.

Resolves Types: Assigns the most specific types that satisfy all constraints.

Example:
haskell
Copy code
```
double x = x * 2
```

The compiler infers that x must be a number since * is used.

The inferred type is:
haskell
Copy code
```
double :: Num a => a -> a
```

Here, Num a => means the function works with any type a that belongs to the Num type class.

Benefits of Type Inference

Concise Code: Developers can omit type annotations for simpler functions, reducing boilerplate.

Static Safety: Types are still checked at compile-time, ensuring reliability.
Flexibility: Functions can automatically adapt to multiple types, enabling polymorphism.

Examples of Type Inference

Basic Function

haskell
Copy code
```
square x = x * x
```

The compiler infers:

haskell
Copy code
```
square :: Num a => a -> a
```

List Functions

haskell
Copy code

addOneToList xs = map (+1) xs

The inferred type:

haskell

Copy code

addOneToList :: Num a => [a] -> [a]

Higher-Order Functions

haskell

Copy code

applyTwice f x = f (f x)

The inferred type:

haskell

Copy code

applyTwice :: (a -> a) -> a -> a

Explicit vs. Inferred Types

While Haskell can infer types, explicitly declaring them is considered good practice:

Improves Readability: Helps others understand your code.
Avoids Ambiguity: Clarifies intent when working with complex types.

Example:

haskell
Copy code
```
-- Explicit type annotation
sumList :: [Int] -> Int
sumList xs = sum xs
```

Limitations of Type Inference

Complex Functions: The compiler may struggle with very complex or ambiguous expressions.
Ambiguity: Without annotations, certain expressions might lead to ambiguous types.

Example:
haskell
Copy code

ambiguous = read "123" -- Compiler needs context to infer type

Conclusion

Type inference in Haskell strikes a balance between flexibility and safety. It simplifies development by reducing the need for explicit type annotations while leveraging Haskell's static typing system to ensure correctness. Explicit type annotations can still complement inferred types for improved clarity and maintainability.

The Power of Strong Typing

Strong typing is one of the most compelling features of Haskell's type system. It ensures that once a type is defined for a variable or function, it cannot be mixed with incompatible types, which dramatically improves program safety and reliability. In Haskell, this means that all types are strictly enforced, and type mismatches are caught at compile time, preventing many common runtime errors.

What is Strong Typing?

Strong typing means that the compiler will not allow operations between incompatible types. For example, trying to add a string to a number, or pass an integer where a string is expected, will result in a compile-time error. Haskell's type system ensures that the types of values are well-defined and strictly checked.

Advantages of Strong Typing in Haskell

Early Error Detection

Since type mismatches are detected at compile time, many potential bugs are caught before the program even runs. This reduces the likelihood of runtime errors and makes debugging easier.

Example:

haskell
Copy code
```
x = "hello"
y = 5
result = x + y  -- Error: cannot add String to Int
```

Safety and Correctness

With strong typing, a variable can only hold values of a particular type, ensuring that functions and operations are performed on compatible data. This guarantees that values will behave as expected, preventing common errors such as invalid calculations or unexpected data manipulation.

Example:

haskell
Copy code
```
multiply :: Int -> Int -> Int
multiply x y = x * y
multiply "hello" 5  -- Error: "hello" is not an Int
```

Improved Readability and Maintainability

Strong typing makes code easier to understand because it clearly defines what type of data a function works with. This explicit type information serves as documentation, making it easier to maintain and modify code over time.

Better Optimization

Strongly-typed languages like Haskell allow the compiler to make optimizations based on known types. Since the types of variables and functions are known at compile-time, the compiler can generate more efficient machine code.

Reusability and Modularity

Functions with well-defined types can be reused in different parts of the code or in different programs. This promotes modularity, as functions are less likely to introduce unexpected behaviors when applied to various inputs of compatible types.

Strong Typing in Haskell vs. Weak Typing

In contrast to weak typing, where type mismatches might only be discovered at runtime or could lead to unexpected behavior, strong typing in Haskell prevents such issues entirely. For example, in weakly-typed languages like JavaScript, you can easily add a string and a number without error, even though this may lead to unexpected results:

Weak Typing Example (JavaScript):

javascript
Copy code
let result = "5" + 5; // Result: "55" (concatenation, not addition)

In Haskell, however, such mismatches are caught at compile time, ensuring that operations like these are not performed:

Strong Typing Example (Haskell):

haskell
Copy code
```
result = "5" + 5  -- Error: Cannot add a String and an Int
```

Type Classes and Polymorphism

Haskell's strong type system also enables powerful abstractions through type classes and polymorphism. Type classes allow you to define functions that can operate on a wide range of types, but with strong guarantees that only compatible types will be used.

For example, the Eq type class allows for equality checks on types that support comparison:

haskell
Copy code
```
class Eq a where
  (==) :: a -> a -> Bool
```

Using the Eq type class, you can define a function that works for any type that implements the Eq class, ensuring type safety:

haskell
Copy code
```
areEqual :: Eq a => a -> a -> Bool
areEqual x y = x == y
```

This is a prime example of how strong typing allows for type-safe polymorphism, where functions can be written generically but still benefit from the strong guarantees of Haskell's type system.

Conclusion

The power of strong typing in Haskell lies in its ability to enforce type correctness at compile time, eliminating a significant class of potential runtime errors and promoting the development of reliable, maintainable, and efficient software. By ensuring that types are strictly adhered to, Haskell's strong typing system enhances code safety, clarity, and reusability, making it a cornerstone of the language's functional programming paradigm.

CHAPTER 6

Algebraic Data Types

Algebraic Data Types (ADTs) are a core feature of Haskell's type system, enabling developers to create complex, expressive, and structured types. ADTs allow you to define types that combine other types in meaningful ways, making them highly suitable for representing real-world data and logic in a type-safe manner.

Types of Algebraic Data Types

Product Types

Product types combine multiple values into a single type. They are analogous to structs or tuples in other languages.

Example:

haskell

Copy code

```
data Point = Point Int Int
```

Here, Point combines two Int values.

Usage:

haskell

Copy code

```
origin :: Point
origin = Point 0 0
```

Sum Types

Sum types (also called union types) allow a value to be one of several alternatives. They are defined using the | symbol.

Example:

haskell

Copy code

data Shape = Circle Float | Rectangle Float Float

Here, a Shape can be a Circle with a radius or a Rectangle with width and height.

Usage:

haskell
Copy code
```
area :: Shape -> Float
area (Circle r) = pi * r * r
area (Rectangle w h) = w * h
```

Recursive Types

Recursive types allow ADTs to reference themselves, making them ideal for defining structures like lists or trees.

Example:

haskell

Copy code

```
data List a = Empty | Cons a (List a)
```

Benefits of ADTs

Type Safety: ADTs ensure that only valid values can be constructed, reducing runtime errors.
Pattern Matching: Haskell's pattern matching works seamlessly with ADTs, simplifying logic and improving code clarity.
Expressiveness: ADTs make it easy to model complex domains using simple, composable types.

Conclusion

Algebraic Data Types are a powerful feature of Haskell, enabling developers to define custom, type-safe structures that enhance the expressiveness and maintainability of their code. By combining product, sum, and recursive types, Haskell allows for robust modeling of real-world data and logic.

Defining Custom Data Types in Haskell

In Haskell, custom data types allow you to define new types that suit the specific needs of your program. This is done using the data keyword, which can be used to create types that combine existing types in flexible ways. Custom data types are a powerful feature of Haskell, enabling better code organization, type safety, and abstraction.

Basic Syntax for Defining Data Types

To define a new data type in Haskell, you use the data keyword followed by the name of the type and its possible constructors.

Syntax:

haskell
Copy code

data TypeName = Constructor1 Type1 Type2 ... | Constructor2 Type1 Type2 ...

TypeName: The name of the new data type.
Constructor: The name of the data constructor used to create values of this type.

Type1, Type2, ...: The types that the constructors take as arguments.

Example: Defining a Simple Data Type

Let's define a simple data type for representing geometric shapes, specifically a Circle and a Rectangle.

haskell
Copy code
data Shape = Circle Float | Rectangle Float Float

In this example:

Shape is the new data type.

Circle is a constructor that takes one argument of type Float (the radius).

Rectangle is a constructor that takes two Float arguments (the width and height).

Creating Values of a Custom Data Type

Once you've defined a custom data type, you can create values of that type using its constructors.

haskell

Copy code

```
-- Create a Circle with radius 5
circle1 :: Shape
circle1 = Circle 5.0

-- Create a Rectangle with width 4 and height 6
rectangle1 :: Shape
rectangle1 = Rectangle 4.0 6.0
```

Pattern Matching with Custom Data Types

Haskell's pattern matching allows you to destructure and handle different constructors of custom data types in a very elegant way. For example, to compute the area of a Shape, we can pattern match on the type of shape.

haskell

Copy code

```
area :: Shape -> Float
area (Circle r) = pi * r * r
area (Rectangle w h) = w * h
```

Here:

area is a function that computes the area of a Shape.

It matches the Circle constructor and uses its radius r to compute the area.

It also matches the Rectangle constructor and uses the width w and height h.

Recursive Data Types

Custom data types can also be recursive, meaning they can reference themselves. This is especially useful for representing structures like lists and trees.

For example, we can define a simple binary tree:

haskell
Copy code
```
data Tree a = Empty | Node a (Tree a) (Tree a)
```

Tree is a data type that holds values of type a (the type of the data in the tree nodes).

Empty represents an empty tree.

Node holds a value of type a and two subtrees (which are also of type Tree a).

Example: Using Recursive Data Types

Let's create a simple tree and define a function to count the number of nodes.

haskell

Copy code

```
-- Define a simple binary tree
myTree :: Tree Int
myTree = Node 1 (Node 2 Empty Empty) (Node 3 Empty Empty)

-- Count the number of nodes in the tree
countNodes :: Tree a -> Int
countNodes Empty = 0
countNodes (Node _ left right) = 1 + countNodes left + countNodes right
```

In this example:

myTree is a simple binary tree with 3 nodes.
countNodes recursively counts the nodes in a tree, using pattern matching to differentiate between an empty tree (Empty) and a node (Node).

Conclusion

Defining custom data types in Haskell is a powerful way to model complex data and logic in a type-safe manner. With Haskell's data keyword, you can create simple or recursive data structures, enabling you to design clean, expressive, and maintainable programs. Custom data types also integrate seamlessly with pattern matching, which simplifies working with them by providing a clear and concise way to deconstruct and manipulate values.

Pattern Matching with Algebraic Data Types

Pattern matching is a fundamental feature of Haskell that allows you to deconstruct and work with Algebraic Data Types (ADTs) in an expressive and concise manner. It enables you to handle different cases of ADTs by matching values against their constructors and extracting the associated data directly.

What is Pattern Matching?

Pattern matching involves testing a value against a series of patterns. When a match is found, the corresponding code is executed. For ADTs, pattern matching is particularly powerful because it provides a clean way to handle each constructor of the type.

Basic Syntax:

haskell

Copy code

```
case expression of
  Pattern1 -> result1
  Pattern2 -> result2
  ...
```

Pattern matching can also be used directly in function definitions, which is common in Haskell.

Example: Pattern Matching with a Simple ADT

Consider an ADT for geometric shapes:

haskell

Copy code

```
data Shape = Circle Float | Rectangle Float Float
```

Here, Shape is an ADT with two constructors:

Circle takes a Float representing the radius.
Rectangle takes two Float values for width and height.
You can use pattern matching to handle these constructors, for example, to calculate the area of a shape:

haskell
Copy code

```
area :: Shape -> Float
area (Circle r) = pi * r * r
area (Rectangle w h) = w * h
```

The (Circle r) pattern matches a Circle and extracts the radius r.
The (Rectangle w h) pattern matches a Rectangle and extracts its width w and height h.

Benefits of Pattern Matching with ADTs

Clarity: It makes the logic for handling different cases of an ADT clear and concise.
Safety: The compiler checks that all constructors are handled, reducing the chance of runtime errors.
Ease of Use: Pattern matching allows you to directly extract and work with the data stored in constructors without additional boilerplate.

Recursive Data Types and Pattern Matching

Pattern matching is especially useful with recursive ADTs, such as lists or trees. For instance, consider a custom list type:

haskell
Copy code
```
data List a = Empty | Cons a (List a)
```

Here:

Empty represents an empty list.

Cons represents a list with a head (an element) and a tail (another list).

You can use pattern matching to sum the elements of a custom list:

haskell

Copy code

```
sumList :: Num a => List a -> a
sumList Empty = 0
sumList (Cons x xs) = x + sumList xs
```

Empty matches an empty list and returns 0.

(Cons x xs) matches a list with a head x and a tail xs, recursively summing the elements.

Pattern Matching with Case Expressions

You can also use case expressions for pattern matching, which is useful for inline logic:

haskell

Copy code

```
describeShape :: Shape -> String
```

```haskell
describeShape shape = case shape of
  Circle _ -> "This is a Circle"
  Rectangle _ _ -> "This is a Rectangle"
```

This is equivalent to the function-based pattern matching but allows more flexibility in certain contexts.

Exhaustive Matching

Haskell requires that all possible patterns for an ADT are handled. If you miss a pattern, the compiler will warn you. For example:

haskell
Copy code
```haskell
describeShape :: Shape -> String
describeShape (Circle _) = "Circle"
-- Missing case for Rectangle will cause a compiler warning!
```

To explicitly handle all cases, you can use a wildcard _ pattern:

haskell
Copy code
```haskell
describeShape :: Shape -> String
describeShape (Circle _) = "Circle"
describeShape _ = "Other shape"
```

Conclusion

Pattern matching with ADTs is one of Haskell's most powerful features, providing a clean and intuitive way to handle complex data types. By matching constructors and extracting their data, you can implement type-safe, readable, and maintainable logic. Whether working with simple or recursive types, pattern matching is a core tool for leveraging the full power of Haskell's functional programming paradigm.

CHAPTER 7

Type Classes and Polymorphism

Haskell's type classes and polymorphism enable the creation of generic, reusable, and type-safe code. Type classes define a set of operations or behaviors that a type must implement, while polymorphism allows these behaviors to work seamlessly across multiple types.

What Are Type Classes?

A type class is a way to define a group of types that share a common set of functions or behaviors. It acts like an interface in object-oriented programming.

Example:
The Eq type class defines equality and inequality for types:

haskell
Copy code

```
class Eq a where
  (==) :: a -> a -> Bool
```

(/=) :: a -> a -> Bool

Any type that wants to be an instance of Eq must implement the (==) and (/=) functions.

Defining Instances of a Type Class

To make a type an instance of a type class, you define how it implements the type class's functions.

Example:

Making a custom type an instance of Eq:

haskell
Copy code
```
data Color = Red | Blue | Green

instance Eq Color where
  Red == Red = True
  Blue == Blue = True
  Green == Green = True
  _ == _ = False
```

Polymorphism with Type Classes

Type classes enable ad-hoc polymorphism, where functions can operate on any type that belongs to a specific type class.

Example:
The show function works with any type that is an instance of the Show class:

haskell
Copy code
```
show :: Show a => a -> String
```

Here, the Show a => constraint specifies that a must implement the Show type class.

Built-in Type Classes

Some common Haskell type classes include:

Eq: For equality comparison.
Ord: For ordering (e.g., <, >, <=).

Show: For converting a value to a string.

Read: For parsing a string into a value.

Num: For numeric types.

Creating Custom Type Classes

You can define your own type classes to abstract over specific behaviors.

Example:

A type class for displaying formatted data:

haskell

Copy code

```
class Formattable a where
  format :: a -> String
```

Creating an instance:

haskell

Copy code

```
instance Formattable Color where
  format Red = "Color: Red"
```

```
format Blue = "Color: Blue"
format Green = "Color: Green"
```

Conclusion

Haskell's type classes and polymorphism provide a powerful mechanism for abstraction and code reuse. By defining shared behaviors through type classes and leveraging polymorphism, developers can write flexible and type-safe functions that work across diverse data types. This combination is a cornerstone of Haskell's type system, enabling expressive and maintainable functional programming.

What are Type Classes?

In Haskell, type classes are a way to define a set of operations or behaviors that can be implemented by different types. They serve as an abstraction mechanism, allowing you to write generic and reusable code. A type class specifies a set of functions or methods that types must implement to become an instance of that class.

Key Features of Type Classes:

Behavior Definition: A type class defines a collection of related functions that a type must implement.
Ad-hoc Polymorphism: Type classes allow functions to work with any type that implements a specific behavior, enabling polymorphism.
Static Type Safety: Haskell enforces at compile time that types implementing a type class provide the required functionality.

Syntax of a Type Class

The general syntax for defining a type class is:

haskell
Copy code
class TypeClassName a where

```
  function1 :: a -> ReturnType
  function2 :: a -> AnotherType -> ReturnType
```

Here:

TypeClassName is the name of the type class.
a is a type variable that represents any type.
function1, function2, etc., are the methods the type class defines.

Example: The Eq Type Class

The Eq type class provides a way to define equality and inequality for types:

haskell
Copy code

```
class Eq a where
  (==) :: a -> a -> Bool
  (/=) :: a -> a -> Bool
```

Any type that is an instance of Eq must define how (==) and (/=) work.

This allows you to compare values of that type for equality.

Making a Type an Instance of a Type Class

To make a type part of a type class, you define how it implements the methods of the class.

Example:

haskell

Copy code

```
data Color = Red | Green | Blue

instance Eq Color where
  Red == Red = True
  Green == Green = True
  Blue == Blue = True
  _ == _ = False
```

Here:

Color is made an instance of the Eq type class.

The == operator is defined for Color values.

Using Type Classes in Functions

Type classes enable constraints in function definitions, specifying that a function works only with types that are instances of a particular type class.

Example:

haskell
Copy code
```
isEqual :: Eq a => a -> a -> Bool
isEqual x y = x == y
```

The Eq a => constraint ensures the function works only with types that are instances of Eq.
This makes the function generic and reusable for any type that supports equality.

Conclusion

Type classes in Haskell provide a powerful mechanism for defining and working with shared behaviors across types. They enable generic programming, allowing you to write reusable and type-safe code while maintaining clarity and abstraction.

Defining and Using Type Classes

Type classes in Haskell provide a framework for defining and enforcing shared behavior across types. They allow developers to write generic and reusable code, enabling functions to work seamlessly with different types that conform to a specific set of rules.

Defining a Type Class

To define a type class, use the class keyword followed by the type class name and its methods.

Syntax:

haskell

Copy code

```
class TypeClassName a where
  method1 :: a -> ReturnType
  method2 :: a -> AnotherType -> ReturnType
```

Here:

TypeClassName is the name of the type class.
a is a type variable representing any type.
method1, method2, etc., are the methods that types must implement to belong to this class.

Example: Defining a Custom Type Class

Let's define a type class Describable for types that can return a description:

haskell
Copy code

```
class Describable a where
  describe :: a -> String
```

This type class requires any instance to implement the describe function.

Making a Type an Instance of a Type Class.

To make a type an instance of a type class, use the instance keyword and define the required methods for the type.

Example: Implementing Describable for a Custom Type

haskell
Copy code
```
data Animal = Dog | Cat | Bird

instance Describable Animal where
   describe Dog  = "This is a dog."
   describe Cat  = "This is a cat."
   describe Bird = "This is a bird."
```

Here:

Animal is a custom data type with three constructors: Dog, Cat, and Bird.
We implement describe for each constructor of Animal.

Using Type Classes in Functions

Type classes allow functions to operate on any type that is an instance of a particular class by specifying constraints.

Example: A Function with Type Class Constraints

haskell
Copy code
```
printDescription :: Describable a => a -> IO ()
printDescription x = putStrLn (describe x)
```

The Describable a => part specifies that the function works for any type a that is an instance of Describable.
You can now call printDescription with any Describable type:
haskell
Copy code

```
main :: IO ()
main = do
  printDescription Dog
  printDescription Cat
```

Built-in Type Classes in Haskell

Haskell provides several built-in type classes, such as:

Eq: For equality (==, /=).
Ord: For ordering (<, >, <=, >=).
Show: For converting a value to a string.
Read: For parsing strings into values.
Num: For numeric types.

Defining a Multi-Parameter Type Class

Haskell also allows defining type classes with multiple parameters.

Example:

haskell

Copy code

```
class Convertible a b where
  convert :: a -> b
```

This defines a relationship between two types (a and b) for conversion.

Implementing Instances:

haskell

Copy code

```
instance Convertible Int String where
  convert x = show x

instance Convertible String Int where
  convert s = read s
```

Advantages of Type Classes

Reusability: Write generic functions that work with different types.

Extensibility: Add new types to existing type classes without modifying the original code.
Static Type Safety: Ensure that only valid types are used with specific functions.
Code Clarity: Encapsulate related behaviors in a clear, modular way.

Conclusion

Defining and using type classes is a fundamental aspect of Haskell programming. By encapsulating shared behaviors and enabling polymorphism, type classes make code more modular, reusable, and maintainable. With a combination of built-in and custom type classes, Haskell developers can leverage the full power of its type system for both small-scale and complex applications.

Polymorphism and Generic Programming in Haskell

Polymorphism and generic programming are central to Haskell's functional programming paradigm. They enable developers to write flexible and reusable code by abstracting operations over different types without sacrificing type safety.

Types of Polymorphism

Haskell supports two primary forms of polymorphism:

Parametric Polymorphism

Allows functions to operate on any type without depending on the specifics of that type.
The same implementation works for all types.

Example:

The length function works for a list of any type:

haskell

Copy code

```
length :: [a] -> Int
```

Here, a is a type variable, indicating that length works for lists of any type.

Ad-hoc Polymorphism (Type Class Polymorphism)

Allows functions to operate on multiple types, but requires each type to implement a specific set of operations defined by a type class.

Example:

The (+) operator works on types that are instances of the Num type class:

haskell

Copy code

```
(+) :: Num a => a -> a -> a
```

The Num a => constraint ensures that a belongs to the Num type class.

Generic Programming in Haskell

Generic programming is about writing code that works for a variety of types while minimizing duplication. Haskell facilitates this through parametric polymorphism and type classes.

Example: A Generic Function

The map function applies a given function to every element in a list, regardless of the element type:

haskell
Copy code
```
map :: (a -> b) -> [a] -> [b]
```
Here:

(a -> b) represents a function that takes an input of type a and returns a value of type b.

The function works generically on lists of any type.

Using Type Classes for Polymorphism

Type classes allow developers to define operations that work generically over any type that satisfies the requirements of a type class.

Example: Polymorphism with Eq

The isEqual function checks equality for any type that implements the Eq type class:

haskell
Copy code
```
isEqual :: Eq a => a -> a -> Bool
isEqual x y = x == y
```

This function works for any type that implements Eq, such as Int, String, or custom types.

Higher-Kinded Types

Haskell's support for higher-kinded types enables generic programming over data structures, such as lists, Maybe, and Either.

Example: The Functor Type Class

The Functor type class provides a generic way to apply a function to values inside a container:

haskell
Copy code
```
class Functor f where
  fmap :: (a -> b) -> f a -> f b
```

Instances of Functor include data structures like Maybe and lists:

haskell
Copy code
```
instance Functor Maybe where
  fmap _ Nothing  = Nothing
  fmap f (Just x) = Just (f x)
```

Benefits of Polymorphism and Generic Programming

Code Reusability: Write functions once and use them for multiple types.
Type Safety: Constraints ensure functions are used only with valid types.
Abstraction: Simplify code by focusing on behavior rather than implementation details.
Flexibility: Combine generic programming with specific type constraints for customized behavior.

Conclusion

Polymorphism and generic programming in Haskell empower developers to create flexible, reusable, and type-safe solutions. Through parametric polymorphism, ad-hoc polymorphism, and type classes, Haskell enables abstraction over types while maintaining clear and robust code. These features are key to building scalable and elegant software in Haskell.

PART IV: FUNCTIONAL COMPOSITION AND HIGHER-ORDER FUNCTIONS

CHAPTER 8

Function Composition and Pipelines

Function composition and pipelines are fundamental concepts in Haskell that allow you to combine smaller functions to create more complex ones while keeping code clean and expressive.

Function Composition

Function composition in Haskell uses the (.) operator, allowing you to chain functions together. The output of one function becomes the input of the next, enabling concise and declarative code.

Syntax:

haskell

Copy code

```
(.) :: (b -> c) -> (a -> b) -> (a -> c)
f . g = \x -> f (g x)
```

Example:

haskell

Copy code

```
double :: Int -> Int
double x = x * 2

increment :: Int -> Int
increment x = x + 1

combined :: Int -> Int
combined = double . increment

-- Usage
result = combined 3  -- Output: 8
```

Here, combined applies increment first and then double.

Pipelines

Pipelines use the (>>>) operator (from the Control.Arrow module) or can be mimicked with reverse function application (& or custom operators). They allow you to express data flow from one operation to the next in a readable, step-by-step manner.

Example using (>>>):

```haskell
Copy code
import Control.Arrow ((>>>))

pipeline :: Int -> Int
pipeline = increment >>> double

result = pipeline 3  -- Output: 8
```

Example with & (from Data.Function):

```haskell
Copy code
import Data.Function ((&))
```

```haskell
result = 3 & increment & double  -- Output: 8
```

Benefits

Readability: Code resembles the flow of operations, making it easier to understand.
Reusability: Individual functions can be tested and reused independently.
Declarative Style: Promotes a clean and functional approach to problem-solving.

Conclusion

Function composition and pipelines simplify function chaining, enhancing code clarity and reusability in Haskell. These tools are key to writing concise and maintainable functional programs.

The Concept of Function Composition

Function composition is a core concept in functional programming and is highly emphasized in Haskell. It refers to combining two or more functions to create a new function, where the output of one function becomes the input to the next. Function composition promotes modular, reusable, and readable code.

The Composition Operator (.)

In Haskell, function composition is performed using the (.) operator. The operator takes two functions as arguments and returns a new function that is their composition.

Definition of (.):

haskell
Copy code
```
(.) :: (b -> c) -> (a -> b) -> (a -> c)
f . g = \x -> f (g x)
```
f and g are functions.
The result of g is passed to f.

Example of Function Composition

Suppose we have two functions:

haskell

Copy code

```
double :: Int -> Int
double x = x * 2

increment :: Int -> Int
increment x = x + 1
```

We can compose them:

haskell

Copy code

```
composedFunction :: Int -> Int
composedFunction = double . increment

result = composedFunction 3  -- Output: 8
```

Here:

increment is applied first, producing 4 from 3.

double is then applied to 4, resulting in 8.

Benefits of Function Composition

Modularity: Individual functions can be written and tested separately.
Reusability: Functions can be reused in different compositions.
Conciseness: Reduces boilerplate code by removing intermediate variables.
Declarative Style: Makes code cleaner and more expressive by focusing on the "what" rather than the "how."

Nested Composition

Function composition can be nested to combine multiple functions:

haskell
Copy code
```
addOneAndSquare :: Int -> Int
addOneAndSquare = square . increment
```

```
square :: Int -> Int
square x = x * x

result = addOneAndSquare 4  -- Output: 25
```

Here, increment is applied first, followed by square.

Real-World Example

Function composition is often used in data transformations, such as string processing:

haskell
Copy code

```
processString :: String -> String
processString = reverse . map toUpper . filter isAlpha
```

filter isAlpha removes non-alphabetic characters.
map toUpper converts all characters to uppercase.
reverse reverses the string.

Conclusion

Function composition is a powerful concept that simplifies combining operations in a concise and readable way. In Haskell, it plays a significant role in building modular, reusable, and declarative code. By chaining smaller functions, developers can create complex transformations with minimal effort and maximum clarity.

Building Complex Operations with Composition

In Haskell, function composition allows you to build complex operations by combining simple, smaller functions. This approach leads to cleaner, more maintainable code that is easy to understand and extend. Rather than writing long, imperative procedures, you can compose functions in a modular and declarative manner.

Combining Simple Functions for Complex Logic
Each function in Haskell is designed to do one thing well. When building complex operations, you start by composing these small, focused functions together.

Example: Complex String Transformation

Suppose we want to process a string by:

Removing non-alphabetic characters.
Converting the string to uppercase.
Reversing the string.

We can compose simple functions to achieve this:

haskell
Copy code
```
import Data.Char (toUpper, isAlpha)

removeNonAlpha :: String -> String
removeNonAlpha = filter isAlpha

toUpperCase :: String -> String
```

```
toUpperCase = map toUpper

reverseString :: String -> String
reverseString = reverse

processString :: String -> String
processString = reverseString . toUpperCase .
removeNonAlpha

result = processString "Haskell 123!" -- Output:
"KSELLAH"
```

Here, the operation is built by composing removeNonAlpha, toUpperCase, and reverseString. Each function handles a single task, and by composing them, we achieve the desired transformation.

Building Pipelines of Operations

Composition is also ideal for building pipelines where data flows through multiple steps of transformations. This is common when processing or transforming data in a sequence of operations.

Example: Numerical Pipeline

Imagine a sequence of mathematical operations:

Square the number.
Add a constant.
Divide by another constant.

We can compose these operations into a single pipeline:

haskell
Copy code
```
square :: Int -> Int
square x = x * x

addConstant :: Int -> Int
addConstant x = x + 5

divideConstant :: Int -> Int
divideConstant x = x `div` 3

pipeline :: Int -> Int
```

pipeline = divideConstant . addConstant . square

result = pipeline 4 -- Output: 5

Here, square 4 = 16, addConstant 16 = 21, and divideConstant 21 = 5. The operations are performed in sequence using composition.

Composing Functions with Different Arities

Haskell allows function composition even with functions that take more than one argument. You can partially apply functions to reduce their arity, then compose the resulting functions.

Example: Function Composition with Multiple Arguments

Suppose we have a function add that takes two arguments, and we want to compose it with another function multiply:

haskell

Copy code

```
add :: Int -> Int -> Int
add x y = x + y

multiply :: Int -> Int -> Int
multiply x y = x * y

addAndMultiply :: Int -> Int -> Int
addAndMultiply = (multiply 2 .) . add

result = addAndMultiply 3 4  -- Output: 14
```

Here:

add 3 4 = 7

Then, multiply 2 7 = 14

Composing with Higher-Order Functions

Haskell allows functions that take other functions as arguments (higher-order functions). This enables more flexible compositions, where the behavior of functions can be customized on the fly.

Example: Applying Functions to Lists

We can compose a function that applies a transformation to each element of a list:

haskell
Copy code
```
transformList :: (a -> b) -> [a] -> [b]
transformList f = map f

transformStringList :: [String] -> [String]
transformStringList = transformList (reverse . toUpperCase)

result = transformStringList ["hello", "world"] -- Output: ["OLLEH","DLROW"]
```

Here, transformList is a higher-order function that takes a function f and a list. We pass a composed function (reverse . toUpperCase) to transform each string in the list.

Combining Functions for Conditional Logic

In more complex cases, you may need to compose functions with conditional logic. By composing basic conditional functions, you can create flexible and reusable decision-making processes.

Example: Conditional Function Composition

haskell

Copy code

```
isEven :: Int -> Bool
isEven x = x `mod` 2 == 0

doubleIfEven :: Int -> Int
doubleIfEven x = if isEven x then x * 2 else x

result1 = doubleIfEven 4  -- Output: 8
result2 = doubleIfEven 5  -- Output: 5
```

Here, the function doubleIfEven is composed using the isEven check to decide whether to double the number or not.

Advantages of Building Complex Operations with Composition

Modularity: By breaking down complex logic into small, reusable functions, you can focus on one task at a time.
Readability: Function composition allows you to express complex operations in a clear and concise manner.
Testability: Smaller functions are easier to test in isolation, ensuring correctness at every step.
Maintainability: Modifications to one part of a system are isolated and don't affect other areas, promoting easier debugging and extension.
Declarative Style: Composition promotes a declarative approach to programming, where you describe what should be done rather than how to do it.

Conclusion

Building complex operations through function composition in Haskell leads to elegant, clean, and maintainable code. By composing small, focused functions into more complex ones, you can easily construct powerful data transformations, handle conditional logic, and create reusable code that is easy to understand and test.

Pipelining Functions in Haskell

Pipelining is a functional programming concept that enables chaining a series of operations, where the output of one function becomes the input to the next. In Haskell, pipelining can be achieved using operators such as (&) (reverse application) or by explicitly passing data through functions. Pipelines provide a clean and readable way to express complex transformations.

The (&) Operator for Pipelining

Haskell provides the (&) operator, available in the Data.Function module, for creating pipelines. This operator reverses the usual function application ($), allowing you to write code in a natural, left-to-right order.

Syntax:

haskell
Copy code
```
(&) :: a -> (a -> b) -> b
x & f = f x
```

The value x is passed to the function f.
Example:

haskell
Copy code
```
import Data.Function ((&))

result :: Int
result = 3 & (+ 1) & (* 2)  -- Output: 8
```

Here, the pipeline:

Adds 1 to 3 (resulting in 4).

Multiplies 4 by 2 (resulting in 8).

Pipelining for List Processing

Pipelines are particularly useful for processing lists with a sequence of transformations.

Example: String Processing Pipeline

haskell

Copy code

```
import Data.Char (toUpper, isAlpha)

processString :: String -> String
processString str = str
  & filter isAlpha
  & map toUpper
  & reverse

result = processString "Haskell 123!" -- Output: "KSELLAH"
```

filter isAlpha removes non-alphabetic characters.

map toUpper converts all characters to uppercase.

reverse reverses the string.

Explicit Pipelining Without Operators

You can also manually pass data through functions to achieve a pipeline effect. While not as concise, this method achieves the same result.

Example:

haskell
Copy code
```
processString :: String -> String
processString str = reverse (map toUpper (filter isAlpha str))

result = processString "Haskell 123!"  -- Output: "KSELLAH"
```

Composing Pipelines with Function

Composition

Pipelines can be combined with function composition (.) for reusable and modular transformations. Instead of applying functions directly to values, you create a composed function that encapsulates the pipeline.

Example:

haskell
Copy code
```
processString :: String -> String
processString = reverse . map toUpper . filter isAlpha

result = processString "Haskell 123!"  -- Output: "KSELLAH"
```
Here, the pipeline is represented as a single composed function.

Real-World Applications of Pipelining

Data Transformation:

Transforming data structures like lists, strings, or custom types using pipelines for readability and efficiency.

ETL (Extract, Transform, Load) Pipelines:
In data processing, pipelines help apply a series of transformations to datasets in a declarative manner.

Function Chaining in APIs:

Haskell's pipelines are used to chain operations in libraries such as conduit or pipes for streaming data processing.

Example: Processing Numbers in a List

haskell
Copy code
```
processNumbers :: [Int] -> [Int]
processNumbers nums = nums
  & filter even
  & map (* 2)
  & take 5

result = processNumbers [1..10]  -- Output: [4, 8, 12, 16, 20]
```

Benefits of Pipelining

Readability: The left-to-right flow of pipelines mirrors how data flows through operations, making code easier to understand.
Declarative Style: Focus on what transformations to apply rather than how to apply them.
Reusability: Functions used in pipelines are modular and can be reused in other contexts.
Reduced Boilerplate: Eliminates intermediate variables, reducing clutter in code.

Conclusion

Pipelining in Haskell simplifies chaining function calls, offering a declarative and readable way to express transformations. By leveraging operators like (&) or using manual pipelines, developers can process data step-by-step in a clear and modular manner. Pipelines are an essential tool for writing elegant and maintainable Haskell code.

CHAPTER 9
Higher-Order Functions

Higher-order functions are a cornerstone of functional programming, including Haskell. These are functions that can take other functions as arguments, return functions as results, or both. They enable a high level of abstraction and modularity, making code reusable and concise.

Characteristics of Higher-Order Functions

Accept Functions as Arguments: They can process functions just like any other data type.
Return Functions as Results: They can generate new functions dynamically.
Enable Abstraction: By working with functions, higher-order functions reduce duplication and promote reusable patterns.

Examples of Higher-Order Functions in Haskell

map: Applies a function to every element in a list.

haskell
Copy code
```
square :: Int -> Int
square x = x * x

result = map square [1, 2, 3, 4] -- Output: [1, 4, 9, 16]
```
filter: Selects elements from a list that satisfy a predicate.

haskell
Copy code
```
isEven :: Int -> Bool
isEven x = x `mod` 2 == 0

result = filter isEven [1, 2, 3, 4] -- Output: [2, 4]
```
foldl and foldr: Accumulate a result by applying a function to elements of a list.

haskell

Copy code

```
sumList :: [Int] -> Int
sumList = foldl (+) 0

result = sumList [1, 2, 3, 4]  -- Output: 10
```

Benefits of Higher-Order Functions

Modularity: Simplifies complex logic by breaking it into reusable components.
Code Reusability: Reduces repetition and encourages general solutions.

Functional Abstraction: Enables expressing operations like mapping, filtering, and reducing at a higher level.

Conclusion

Higher-order functions make Haskell powerful and expressive. By abstracting logic and enabling function manipulation, they are vital tools for writing clean, concise, and modular functional programs.

What Are Higher-Order Functions?

Higher-order functions are functions that operate on other functions. Specifically, they can either:

Take other functions as arguments, or
Return functions as results.

This ability makes higher-order functions a powerful feature in functional programming, allowing for flexible and modular code.

Characteristics of Higher-Order Functions

Function Arguments: They accept other functions as input, enabling custom behavior.
Function Outputs: They can generate and return new functions dynamically.
Abstraction: They encapsulate patterns of computation, reducing code repetition.

Examples of Higher-Order Functions

map: Applies a given function to every element in a list.

haskell

Copy code

```
double :: Int -> Int
double x = x * 2

result = map double [1, 2, 3]  -- Output: [2, 4, 6]
```

filter: Selects elements from a list based on a predicate function.

haskell

Copy code

```
isOdd :: Int -> Bool
isOdd x = x `mod` 2 /= 0

result = filter isOdd [1, 2, 3, 4]  -- Output: [1, 3]
```

Returning Functions:

haskell

Copy code

```
makeMultiplier :: Int -> (Int -> Int)
```

```
makeMultiplier n = \x -> n * x

multiplierBy2 = makeMultiplier 2
result = multiplierBy2 5  -- Output: 10
```

Benefits of Higher-Order Functions

Code Reusability: Generic operations like mapping or filtering can be reused with different logic.
Modularity: They encourage breaking problems into smaller, reusable components.
Flexibility: They adapt behavior dynamically by taking functions as input.

Conclusion

Higher-order functions are fundamental in Haskell and functional programming, allowing developers to write concise, modular, and expressive code by abstracting and reusing common patterns of computation.

Using Higher-Order Functions for Abstraction

Higher-order functions enable abstraction by encapsulating common patterns of computation and reusing them across different contexts. In Haskell, they allow developers to write concise and expressive code by focusing on what needs to be done rather than how it is implemented.

Why Use Abstraction?

Reduce Repetition: Avoid duplicating similar code.
Increase Readability: Focus on the logic, not the implementation details.
Enhance Reusability: Generalize solutions for broader use cases.

Examples of Abstraction with

Higher-Order Functions

Abstracting Iteration with map

Instead of writing loops or manual list processing, use map to apply a function to every element.

haskell
Copy code

```
doubleAll :: [Int] -> [Int]
doubleAll = map (* 2)

result = doubleAll [1, 2, 3] -- Output: [2, 4, 6]
```

The logic of "applying a function to each element" is abstracted by map.

Abstracting Filtering with filter

Filter lists based on conditions without writing explicit loops.

haskell
Copy code

```
keepEvens :: [Int] -> [Int]
keepEvens = filter even
```

```haskell
result = keepEvens [1, 2, 3, 4] -- Output: [2, 4]
```

The operation of selecting elements is generalized by filter.

Abstracting Accumulation with foldr

Summing a list or calculating a product can be abstracted with foldr.

haskell
Copy code
```haskell
sumList :: [Int] -> Int
sumList = foldr (+) 0

result = sumList [1, 2, 3, 4] -- Output: 10
```
foldr abstracts the pattern of combining elements in a list with a binary function.

Custom Abstraction with Function Arguments

Define your own higher-order function to abstract repetitive patterns.

haskell
Copy code

```
applyTwice :: (a -> a) -> a -> a
applyTwice f x = f (f x)

result = applyTwice (+1) 3  -- Output: 5
```

Here, applyTwice abstracts the concept of applying a function twice.

Benefits of Abstraction with Higher-Order Functions

Simplicity: Focus on high-level logic rather than low-level details.
Modularity: Break down problems into reusable components.
Expressiveness: Write clear and concise code, reducing cognitive load.

Real-World Applications

Data Transformation: Abstract data processing pipelines using map, filter, and fold.
Custom DSLs: Create domain-specific abstractions by defining higher-order functions.
UI Logic: Abstract common user interaction patterns in GUI libraries.

Conclusion

Higher-order functions are powerful tools for abstraction in Haskell. By capturing recurring patterns and making code reusable and concise, they enable developers to write clean, modular, and expressive programs.

Common Higher-Order Functions in Haskell

Higher-order functions are central to Haskell's functional programming paradigm. They allow developers to manipulate and process data more effectively by abstracting common patterns. Here are some widely used higher-order functions in Haskell:

1. map

Applies a given function to every element of a list.

Use Case: Transform data in a list.

Example:

haskell

Copy code

```
square :: Int -> Int
square x = x * x

result = map square [1, 2, 3, 4]  -- Output: [1, 4, 9, 16]
```

2. filter

Selects elements from a list that satisfy a given predicate.

Use Case: Extract subsets of data based on conditions.
Example:
haskell
Copy code

```
isEven :: Int -> Bool
isEven x = x `mod` 2 == 0

result = filter isEven [1, 2, 3, 4]  -- Output: [2, 4]
```

3. foldr and foldl

Reduce a list to a single value by applying a binary function.

Use Case: Summing, finding the product, or concatenating elements.
Examples:
haskell
Copy code

```
-- Using foldr (right-associative)
sumList :: [Int] -> Int
sumList = foldr (+) 0
```

```
-- Using foldl (left-associative)
productList :: [Int] -> Int
productList = foldl (*) 1

result1 = sumList [1, 2, 3, 4]       -- Output: 10
result2 = productList [1, 2, 3, 4]  -- Output: 24
```

4. zipWith

Combines two lists element-wise using a binary function.

Use Case: Perform pairwise operations on two lists.

Example:
haskell
Copy code

```
addPairs :: [Int] -> [Int] -> [Int]
addPairs = zipWith (+)

result = addPairs [1, 2, 3] [4, 5, 6]  -- Output: [5, 7, 9]
```

5. takeWhile and dropWhile

Work with elements of a list based on a predicate.

takeWhile: Extracts elements from the start of the list while the condition holds.

haskell

Copy code

```
takeWhile (< 5) [1, 2, 3, 6, 4]  -- Output: [1, 2, 3]
```

dropWhile: Discards elements from the start of the list while the condition holds.

haskell

Copy code

```
dropWhile (< 5) [1, 2, 3, 6, 4]  -- Output: [6, 4]
```

6. iterate

Generates an infinite list by repeatedly applying a function.

Use Case: Create sequences or patterns.

Example:

haskell

Copy code

```haskell
result = take 5 (iterate (* 2) 1)  -- Output: [1, 2, 4, 8, 16]
```

7. (.) (Function Composition)

Composes two functions into one.

Use Case: Chain operations in a concise way.

Example:

haskell

Copy code

```haskell
double :: Int -> Int
double x = x * 2

increment :: Int -> Int
increment x = x + 1
```

```haskell
result = (increment . double) 3  -- Output: 7
```

8. $ (Function Application)

Applies a function to an argument, often used to reduce parentheses.

Use Case: Simplify nested function calls.
Example:
haskell
Copy code

```haskell
result = sum $ map (* 2) [1, 2, 3]  -- Output: 12
```

9. flip

Reverses the order of arguments for a function.

Use Case: Adapt functions to match different argument orders.
Example:
haskell

Copy code

```
subtractFlipped = flip (-)

result = subtractFlipped 5 10  -- Output: 5
```

10. curry and uncurry

Convert between curried and uncurried forms of a function.

Use Case: Change how arguments are passed to a function.

Example:

haskell

Copy code

```haskell
add :: (Int, Int) -> Int
add (x, y) = x + y

curriedAdd = curry add
result = curriedAdd 1 2  -- Output: 3
```

Conclusion

These higher-order functions are essential tools in Haskell, abstracting common patterns and enabling concise, reusable, and elegant solutions. Mastering them is key to effective functional programming.

PART V: LAZY EVALUATION AND PERFORMANCE

CHAPTER 10
Introduction to Lazy Evaluation

Lazy evaluation is a key feature of Haskell, where expressions are not evaluated until their values are actually needed. This approach allows Haskell to work with potentially infinite data structures, delay computations, and optimize performance by avoiding unnecessary calculations.

Key Characteristics of Lazy Evaluation

Call-by-Need: Expressions are evaluated only once, when required, and their results are cached for future use.
Infinite Structures: Enables the creation and manipulation of infinite lists or streams.
Efficiency: Avoids unnecessary computations, leading to perfor
mance improvements in some scenarios.

Example: Infinite List

Haskell's lazy evaluation allows the following to work seamlessly:

haskell

Copy code

```
infiniteList = [1..]  -- Infinite list of integers
take 5 infiniteList   -- Output: [1, 2, 3, 4, 5]
```

Here, only the first 5 elements of the infinite list are evaluated.

Benefits of Lazy Evaluation

Modularity: Write functions without worrying about when computations occur.

Performance: Improves efficiency by evaluating only what's needed.

Expressiveness: Enables constructs like infinite lists and delayed computations.

Conclusion

Lazy evaluation is a powerful concept that distinguishes Haskell from many other programming languages, enabling flexibility and performance optimizations in functional programming.

How Lazy Evaluation Works

Lazy evaluation in Haskell is a method of delaying computation until the value is actually needed. This mechanism allows for efficient memory usage, avoiding unnecessary computations, and handling infinite data structures seamlessly. Here's a detailed look at how it works:

Key Mechanisms of Lazy Evaluation

Thunk Creation:

A thunk is a deferred computation.

Instead of evaluating an expression immediately, Haskell creates a thunk to represent the unevaluated computation.

Example:

haskell

Copy code

```
let x = 5 + 3
```

Here, x is not computed immediately but represented as a thunk.

Evaluation on Demand:

When the value of a thunk is needed, it is evaluated.

Example:

haskell

Copy code

```
let x = 5 + 3
print x  -- This triggers the evaluation of `x`, producing 8
```

Memoization:

Once a thunk is evaluated, its result is stored (cached) to avoid re-evaluating the same computation.

Example:

haskell

Copy code

```
let x = expensiveComputation
print x
print x  -- The result is reused; `expensiveComputation` is not called again
```

Example of Lazy Evaluation

Consider working with an infinite list:

haskell

Copy code

```
numbers = [1..]       -- Infinite list
```

result = take 5 numbers -- Only the first 5 elements are computed

In this example:

The infinite list numbers is represented as a thunk.
When take 5 is applied, Haskell evaluates only the first 5 elements and ignores the rest.

Lazy Evaluation in Function Arguments

Haskell's lazy evaluation extends to function arguments, allowing the use of unevaluated expressions:

haskell
Copy code

```
lazyFunction :: Int -> Int -> Int
lazyFunction x y = x

result = lazyFunction 5 (expensiveComputation) -- `expensiveComputation` is never evaluated
```

Here, y is not computed because it is not used in the function body.

Benefits of Lazy Evaluation

Handling Infinite Structures:

Allows safe operations on infinite lists, streams, or sequences.

Performance Optimization:

Avoids unnecessary calculations.
Reduces memory usage by evaluating only required expressions.

Improved Modularity:

Promotes separating computation from its usage, enabling more reusable code.

Conclusion

Lazy evaluation is a cornerstone of Haskell's design, enabling a unique approach to computation. By deferring evaluations and using thunks and memoization, Haskell achieves high efficiency and expressiveness, making it ideal for functional programming tasks.

Benefits and Drawbacks of Lazy Evaluation

Lazy evaluation in Haskell offers several advantages, but it also comes with some potential downsides. Understanding both sides is crucial for writing efficient, effective functional programs.

Benefits of Lazy Evaluation

Improved Performance Through Avoiding Unnecessary Computations

Lazy evaluation only computes values when they are needed, which can significantly reduce the overhead of unnecessary computations.

Example: If a large data structure is created but only a small portion is used, lazy evaluation will only compute the necessary part.

Handling Infinite Data Structures

Lazy evaluation allows the definition and manipulation of infinite data structures. For example, you can define an infinite list of numbers and only process a finite portion of it.

Example:

haskell
Copy code
```
nums = [1..]  -- An infinite list of integers
take 5 nums   -- Only the first 5 elements are computed
```

Modularity and Separation of Concerns

With lazy evaluation, functions can be written in a more modular way, without worrying about when

computations will occur. This can lead to cleaner and more readable code.
Example: You can define a complex computation but delay its evaluation until absolutely necessary.

Memory Efficiency

By only storing evaluated portions of data, Haskell can manage memory efficiently, reducing the risk of unnecessary memory consumption.
Example: A large list is created, but only the first few elements are computed and stored.

Non-Strict Evaluation for Composability

Lazy evaluation allows functions to compose more easily, as operations on unevaluated expressions can be composed without forcing immediate evaluation.

Example:

haskell
Copy code

filter even (map (*2) [1..10]) -- Evaluates only necessary portions of the list

Drawbacks of Lazy Evaluation

Space Leaks (Memory Inefficiency)

Lazy evaluation can sometimes lead to space leaks, where thunks (deferred computations) accumulate in memory because they were never evaluated or used.
If a program creates many unevaluated thunks, it can consume excessive memory, leading to poor performance or even memory exhaustion.

Example:

haskell
Copy code
-- Creating an infinite list that is never fully consumed can lead to memory issues
let xs = [1..] -- Infinite list
let ys = take 5 xs -- The first 5 elements are evaluated, but xs still holds a reference to the whole list

Unpredictability of Performance

Since evaluation is deferred, the actual performance of a program can be harder to predict. Thunks may be evaluated at unexpected times, potentially causing delays or performance bottlenecks.
Example: If a program evaluates a large structure all at once after a long period of time, it can result in long pauses or delays.

Increased Complexity in Debugging

Lazy evaluation can make debugging more difficult because it may be unclear when or why certain expressions are evaluated. This can lead to unpredictable behavior or errors that are hard to trace.
Example: Identifying the root cause of memory leaks or excessive computation can be tricky since the program may not evaluate certain parts until later.

Delayed Error Detection

Errors in lazy-evaluated expressions may not be detected until the point of evaluation, which can make debugging harder, as errors may not appear until much later in the program's execution.
Example: A division by zero in a lazy expression won't throw an error until the program actually tries to evaluate that expression.

Complexity in Optimization

While lazy evaluation can provide performance benefits in many cases, it can also make certain optimizations harder. For instance, some forms of strict evaluation (evaluating values immediately) might lead to better performance in specific contexts, but lazy evaluation may not allow for such optimizations.

Conclusion

Lazy evaluation is a powerful feature in Haskell that allows for efficient memory usage, handling of infinite data structures, and better modularity. However, it also introduces challenges such as potential space leaks, unpredictability in performance, and increased debugging complexity. By understanding the trade-offs, developers can leverage lazy evaluation effectively while mitigating its drawbacks.

Controlling Laziness in Haskell

While laziness is a powerful feature in Haskell, it is not always desirable or efficient in every situation. Fortunately, Haskell provides several mechanisms to control laziness, allowing developers to fine-tune when and how evaluation happens. This control over laziness can help mitigate performance issues such as space leaks and unpredictable behavior.

1. Strict Evaluation with seq

The seq function forces the evaluation of an expression before proceeding to the next. It is often used to control when expressions are evaluated, ensuring they are evaluated strictly rather than lazily.

Example:

haskell
Copy code
```
strictExample :: Int -> Int -> Int
strictExample x y = x `seq` (y + 1)  -- Forces evaluation of x before evaluating (y + 1)
```

In the above example, x is evaluated immediately (strictly), whereas y + 1 is evaluated lazily.

Usage:

Preventing Space Leaks: Using seq can help avoid memory issues caused by accumulating thunks by ensuring parts of the computation are evaluated earlier.
Improving Performance: In cases where deferred evaluation leads to inefficient use of memory, seq can be used to force intermediate computations and reduce overhead.

2. Strict Data Types

Haskell allows you to define strict data types, where the fields of a data structure are evaluated immediately upon creation. This can be done using the ! symbol in data type definitions.

Example:
haskell
Copy code

```
data StrictPair = StrictPair !Int !Int
```

Here, both Int values will be evaluated strictly when a StrictPair is created, avoiding the creation of thunks for the fields.

Usage:

Avoiding Thunks: By marking fields as strict, you can prevent the creation of unevaluated thunks for each field of a data structure, improving memory efficiency and reducing space leaks.

3. The bang patterns (!)

In addition to strict data types, Haskell provides bang patterns (!), which force strict evaluation of function arguments. These can be applied in function definitions to ensure that arguments are evaluated before they are used in the function body.

Example:

haskell
Copy code
```
sumStrict :: Int -> Int -> Int
sumStrict !x !y = x + y
```

Here, x and y are strictly evaluated before they are added together, ensuring that no thunks are generated for these arguments.

Usage:

Strict Evaluation of Function Arguments: Use bang patterns to control the evaluation of function arguments, ensuring they are evaluated immediately and avoiding lazy evaluation in critical parts of the program.

4. The deepseq Function

The deepseq function is used to force the evaluation of a value, including all of its components, deeply. It ensures that not just the top-level value, but also all its substructures, are fully evaluated.

Example:

haskell

Copy code

```
import Control.DeepSeq

deepExample :: (NFData a) => a -> a -> a
deepExample x y = x `deepseq` y `deepseq` (x + y)
```

Here, deepseq ensures that both x and y are evaluated to their deepest form before the final result is computed.

Usage:

Evaluating Complex Structures: When working with complex, nested data structures, deepseq can be used to ensure that all levels of the structure are fully evaluated, preventing thunks from accumulating at deeper levels.

5. Strictness Annotations in Functions

Haskell provides the ability to use strictness annotations to specify that certain functions or arguments should be evaluated strictly. For example, using ! in function definitions ensures that arguments are evaluated immediately.

Example:

haskell
Copy code
```
sumStrict :: !Int -> !Int -> Int
sumStrict x y = x + y
```

The ! here indicates that both x and y are evaluated strictly before performing the addition.

Usage:

Improving Performance: Strictness annotations can be used to optimize performance when working with large data sets or computationally intensive tasks, as they prevent unnecessary lazy evaluations.

6. Using Control.Lazy for More Control

Haskell's Control.Lazy module provides functions for working with lazy lists in a controlled way. These functions can help optimize laziness, especially when dealing with large or infinite lists.

Example:

haskell
Copy code

```
import Control.Lazy
-- Using `take` and `force` to control evaluation
forceEvaluation :: [Int] -> Int
forceEvaluation list = force (take 10 list) -- Forces evaluation of the first 10 elements
```

This allows developers to control exactly when certain parts of a lazy structure are evaluated.

Conclusion

While lazy evaluation offers numerous benefits, it can also introduce inefficiencies if not controlled carefully. Haskell provides several tools, such as seq, strict data types, bang patterns, deepseq, and strictness annotations, to give developers control over evaluation. By using these techniques, developers can avoid issues like space leaks and achieve better performance in their Haskell programs.

CHAPTER 11:
Performance Optimization in Haskell

Haskell's lazy evaluation and strong type system allow for expressive and concise code but can introduce performance challenges if not managed effectively. Optimizing performance in Haskell involves leveraging strictness, efficient data structures, and profiling tools.

Key Techniques for Optimization

Control Laziness

Use seq or deepseq to force strict evaluation and avoid space leaks caused by unevaluated thunks.

Example:
haskell
Copy code

```
result = x `seq` y + z  -- Forces evaluation of `x` before computing `y + z`
```

Strict Data Structures

Use strict versions of data structures (e.g., Data.Map.Strict) to ensure that stored values are evaluated immediately, reducing memory overhead.

Efficient Algorithms and Data Structures

Choose algorithms and libraries optimized for performance. For example, use Vector instead of lists for numerical computations as it provides better cache performance.

Profiling and Benchmarking

Use tools like GHC Profiler and Criterion to identify bottlenecks. Profiling helps focus optimization efforts on performance-critical parts of the code.

Inlining and Specialization

Use compiler pragmas like INLINE and SPECIALIZE to guide the compiler in generating optimized code for frequently used functions.

Parallelism and Concurrency

Use Haskell's parallel programming libraries (e.g., Control.Parallel or Async) to take advantage of multicore processors.

Memory Management

Minimize memory usage by using strict evaluation and compact representations, and avoid creating unnecessary intermediate data structures.

Avoiding Overheads from Lazy Evaluation

Use strict folds (foldl') instead of lazy folds (foldl) for accumulating results efficiently without building large thunks.

Conclusion

Performance optimization in Haskell involves understanding and balancing its lazy nature with explicit strictness where necessary. Profiling, efficient data structures, and parallelism are key tools for creating high-performance Haskell applications.

Understanding Space and Time Complexity

Space and time complexity are critical concepts in computer science that measure the efficiency of algorithms. They help developers evaluate how an algorithm scales with input size, guiding decisions about performance optimization and resource usage.

1. Time Complexity

Time complexity measures the amount of time an algorithm takes to complete as a function of its input size. It is typically expressed using Big-O notation, which describes the upper bound of an algorithm's growth rate.

Common Time Complexities:

O(1): Constant time; the operation takes the same time regardless of input size.
O(log n): Logarithmic time; performance scales logarithmically with input size, e.g., binary search.
O(n): Linear time; performance scales directly with input size, e.g., iterating through a list.
O(n^2): Quadratic time; performance scales with the square of input size, e.g., nested loops.

Example in Haskell:

haskell
Copy code
```
-- Linear time complexity
sumList :: [Int] -> Int
sumList = foldl' (+) 0  -- Processes each element once
(O(n))
```

2. Space Complexity

Space complexity measures the amount of memory an algorithm uses as a function of its input size. This includes:

Fixed Space: Memory required regardless of input size (e.g., variables, constants).
Dynamic Space: Memory required for input, output, and intermediate computations.

Common Factors:

Data structures (e.g., lists, arrays).
Recursive calls (stack space).

Example in Haskell:
haskell
Copy code

```
-- Space complexity with recursive call stack
factorial :: Int -> Int
factorial 0 = 1
```

factorial n = n * factorial (n - 1) -- Creates a stack frame for each call

3. Haskell-Specific Considerations

Haskell's lazy evaluation adds unique dimensions to complexity analysis:

Thunks: Unevaluated expressions can accumulate, increasing memory usage (space complexity).
Avoiding Space Leaks: Use strict evaluation (seq or deepseq) to prevent excessive memory consumption.

Example:

haskell
Copy code
```haskell
-- Space leak due to laziness
sumLazy :: [Int] -> Int
sumLazy = foldl (+) 0  -- Accumulates thunks, causing high space complexity
```

```
-- Strict version
sumStrict :: [Int] -> Int
sumStrict = foldl' (+) 0  -- Forces evaluation, reducing memory usage
```

4. Balancing Trade-offs

Algorithms with better time complexity may use more memory (e.g., caching results).
Choosing between lazy and strict evaluation can impact both space and time complexity.

Conclusion
Understanding space and time complexity is crucial for designing efficient algorithms. In Haskell, developers must consider both traditional complexity measures and the nuances introduced by lazy evaluation. Profiling and testing are essential for optimizing real-world applications.

Optimizing Functional Code for Speed and Memory Efficiency

Functional programming emphasizes immutability, pure functions, and declarative patterns, which can lead to elegant and maintainable code. However, without proper optimization, functional code can sometimes be slower or consume excessive memory. Optimizing functional code requires understanding performance trade-offs and using specific techniques to balance speed and memory efficiency.

1. Avoiding Space Leaks

Space leaks occur when unevaluated expressions (thunks) accumulate, consuming excessive memory.

Use Strict Evaluation: Replace lazy functions like foldl with strict versions like foldl'.

Control Laziness: Use seq or deepseq to force evaluation of intermediate results.

Example:

haskell
Copy code
```
-- Lazy evaluation causing space leaks
lazySum :: [Int] -> Int
lazySum = foldl (+) 0  -- Builds thunks, increasing memory usage

-- Optimized with strict evaluation
strictSum :: [Int] -> Int
strictSum = foldl' (+) 0 -- Forces immediate evaluation
```

2. Use Efficient Data Structures

Choosing the right data structure can drastically improve performance:

Lazy vs. Strict Data Structures: Use strict versions (e.g., Data.Map.Strict) when laziness is unnecessary.
Vectors: Replace linked lists with Data.Vector for better cache performance in numerical computations.
Immutable Structures: Opt for specialized structures like finger trees for efficient updates.

3. Optimize Recursive Functions

Recursive functions, a hallmark of functional programming, can be optimized for speed and memory:

Tail Recursion: Ensure recursion is tail-recursive to avoid stack overflow and enable compiler optimizations.
Accumulators: Use accumulators to make recursive functions strict and efficient.

Example:

haskell
Copy code
-- Non-tail-recursive factorial

```haskell
factorial :: Int -> Int
factorial 0 = 1
factorial n = n * factorial (n - 1)

-- Tail-recursive factorial
factorialTail :: Int -> Int
factorialTail n = go n 1
  where
    go 0 acc = acc
    go n acc = go (n - 1) (n * acc)
```

4. Use Function Composition and Pipelines

Reduce intermediate data structures by combining functions using composition or pipelines. This minimizes memory usage and improves readability.

Example:
haskell
Copy code

```haskell
-- With intermediate list
processData :: [Int] -> [Int]
```

processData xs = map (* 2) (filter even xs)

-- Optimized with composition
processDataOptimized :: [Int] -> [Int]
processDataOptimized = map (* 2) . filter even

5. Leverage Parallelism and Concurrency

Haskell provides powerful tools for parallel and concurrent programming:

Use par and pseq for fine-grained parallelism.
Use libraries like Control.Parallel or async to take advantage of multicore systems.

Example:

haskell
Copy code
import Control.Parallel.Strategies

parallelSum :: [Int] -> Int

```
parallelSum xs = a `par` b `pseq` (a + b)
  where
    (ys, zs) = splitAt (length xs `div` 2) xs
    a = sum ys
    b = sum zs
```

6. Profiling and Benchmarking

Use tools like GHC Profiler and Criterion to identify bottlenecks:

Heap Profiling: Detect and eliminate space leaks.
Time Profiling: Identify slow functions and optimize them.

Example:
bash
Copy code

```
# Compile with profiling
ghc -prof -fprof-auto -rtsopts -o myProgram myProgram.hs
```

```
# Run with profiling enabled
./myProgram +RTS -hc -p
```

7. Inlining and Specialization

Guide the compiler to optimize frequently used functions:

Inlining: Use INLINE pragmas to replace function calls with their definitions.
Specialization: Use SPECIALIZE pragmas to optimize generic functions for specific types.

Example:
haskell
Copy code

```
{-# INLINE add #-}
add :: Int -> Int -> Int
add x y = x + y
```

8. Optimize Garbage Collection

Haskell's garbage collector can affect performance:

Minimize the creation of short-lived objects.
Profile memory usage and adjust runtime flags (e.g., +RTS -A<size>).

Conclusion

Optimizing functional code for speed and memory efficiency in Haskell involves managing laziness, choosing the right data structures, writing efficient recursive functions, and leveraging parallelism. By using profiling tools and understanding Haskell's runtime behavior, developers can fine-tune their code for high performance while retaining functional elegance.

Common Performance Pitfalls in Haskell

Haskell's unique features, like lazy evaluation, immutability, and type inference, make it a powerful language but can also lead to subtle performance issues if not used carefully. Here are some common pitfalls and strategies to avoid them.

1. Space Leaks

Problem: Accumulation of unevaluated expressions (thunks) in memory, causing high memory usage.
Example: Using foldl instead of foldl' creates a chain of unevaluated additions.

Solution:
Use strict evaluation functions like foldl' from Data.List.
Apply seq or deepseq to force evaluation when needed.

haskell
Copy code
```haskell
import Data.List (foldl')

-- Lazy version causing space leak
sumLazy :: [Int] -> Int
```

```
sumLazy = foldl (+) 0

-- Strict version avoiding space leak
sumStrict :: [Int] -> Int
sumStrict = foldl' (+) 0
```

2. Excessive Laziness

Problem: Over-reliance on laziness can result in unexpected performance issues, such as delayed computation or increased memory usage.
Example: Deferring computations unnecessarily.

Solution:
Be explicit about when laziness is necessary.
Use strict data structures (e.g., Data.Map.Strict) where appropriate.

3. Inefficient Data Structures

Problem: Using lists instead of more efficient structures like Vector or Array for numerical or large-scale data processing.
Example: Lists are less cache-friendly and require more memory for random access.

Solution:

Use Data.Vector or Data.Array for efficient storage and manipulation of large datasets.

4. Non-Tail-Recursive Functions

Problem: Recursive functions that are not tail-recursive can cause stack overflows.

Example:

haskell
Copy code
```
-- Non-tail-recursive
factorial :: Int -> Int
```

```haskell
factorial 0 = 1
factorial n = n * factorial (n - 1)
```

Solution:

Rewrite functions to be tail-recursive.

haskell

Copy code

```haskell
-- Tail-recursive version
factorialTail :: Int -> Int
factorialTail n = go n 1
  where
    go 0 acc = acc
    go n acc = go (n - 1) (n * acc)
```

5. Inefficient Use of String

Problem: Using String for text processing can lead to poor performance since it's a linked list of characters.

Example: Operations on String are slower compared to more efficient types.

Solution:

Use Text from Data.Text or ByteString from Data.ByteString for text-heavy applications.

6. Overhead from Generalization

Problem: Writing overly generic code can cause the compiler to generate inefficient intermediate representations.

Solution:
Use type specialization when performance is critical.
Apply the SPECIALIZE pragma for frequently used functions.

7. Improper Use of Parallelism

Problem: Incorrect or excessive use of parallelism can lead to overhead that negates performance gains.
Example: Using par without properly splitting tasks.

Solution:

Ensure tasks are computationally intensive enough to justify parallelism.
Profile parallel performance using tools like GHC's ThreadScope.

8. Unoptimized Garbage Collection

Problem: Excessive memory allocation can lead to frequent garbage collection pauses.

Solution:

Minimize intermediate data structures.
Tune garbage collector settings using runtime options (e.g., +RTS -A<size>).

9. Inefficient Pattern Matching
Problem: Writing exhaustive or redundant patterns can slow down pattern-matching logic.

Solution:

Write concise and specific patterns.
Use case expressions for better clarity and performance in some contexts.

10. Ignoring Profiling Tools

Problem: Guessing performance bottlenecks instead of relying on profiling data can lead to wasted optimization efforts.

Solution:

Use GHC profiling tools to analyze time and memory usage.
Benchmark critical parts of the code with libraries like Criterion.

Conclusion

Performance pitfalls in Haskell often stem from its lazy evaluation model, choice of data structures, and improper handling of recursion and parallelism. By understanding these pitfalls and using tools and techniques like strict evaluation, efficient data types, and profiling, developers can write Haskell code that is both elegant and performant.

PART VI: MONADS AND FUNCTIONAL EFFECTS

CHAPTER 12

Understanding Monads

Monads are a foundational concept in functional programming and Haskell, providing a way to structure computations and handle side effects while maintaining purity. They can be thought of as design patterns that allow chaining operations in a predictable and composable way.

Key Characteristics of Monads:

Type Constructor: A Monad is a type constructor, like Maybe, Either, or IO, that wraps values.
Unit Function (return or pure): Injects a value into the monadic context.

Bind Operator (>>=): Chains computations by unwrapping a monad, applying a function, and re-wrapping the result.

Monad Laws

Monads must satisfy three laws to ensure consistent behavior:

Left Identity: return x >>= f is equivalent to f x.
Right Identity: m >>= return is equivalent to m.
Associativity: (m >>= f) >>= g is equivalent to m >>= (\x -> f x >>= g).

Example: The Maybe Monad

The Maybe type represents computations that might fail.

Nothing represents failure.
Just x represents success with a value x.

Example Code:

haskell

Copy code

```
safeDivide :: Int -> Int -> Maybe Int
safeDivide _ 0 = Nothing
safeDivide x y = Just (x `div` y)

result :: Maybe Int
result = Just 10 >>= (\x -> safeDivide x 2) >>= (\y ->
safeDivide y 2)
-- Output: Just 2
```

Monads simplify error handling, state management, and side effects, making them essential for writing clean and modular Haskell programs.

What is a Monad?

A Monad is an abstraction in functional programming that represents computations as a series of steps. It provides a structure to handle values and operations, especially when dealing with side effects like input/output, state, or exceptions, while maintaining functional purity.

Key Components of a Monad

Type Constructor: A Monad is a type constructor that defines a context for values. For example, Maybe provides a context for optional values, and IO provides a context for input/output actions.

return (or pure): A function that takes a value and wraps it in the monadic context.

Example: return 5 wraps the value 5 in a monad like Just 5 (for Maybe) or IO 5.
Bind Operator (>>=): A function that chains monadic computations by applying a function to a monadic value.

It allows the output of one computation to be used as the input to the next.

Example: Just 5 >>= (\x -> Just (x + 1)) evaluates to Just 6.

Monad Laws

Monads follow three key laws to ensure consistent behavior:

Left Identity: Wrapping a value in a monad and then applying a function is equivalent to directly applying the function.

return x >>= f is the same as f x.

Right Identity: Applying the return function to a monad does not change it.

m >>= return is the same as m.

Associativity: The order of chaining does not matter as long as the sequence is preserved.

(m >>= f) >>= g is the same as m >>= (\x -> f x >>= g).

Practical Example: The Maybe Monad

The Maybe monad is used for computations that may fail. It either holds a value (Just x) or represents failure (Nothing).

Example Code:

haskell
Copy code
```
safeDivide :: Int -> Int -> Maybe Int
safeDivide _ 0 = Nothing
safeDivide x y = Just (x `div` y)

result :: Maybe Int
result = Just 10 >>= (\x -> safeDivide x 2) >>= (\y -> safeDivide y 2)
-- Output: Just 2
```

Why Are Monads Important?

Monads allow developers to:

Compose computations in a clean and predictable way.
Handle side effects like I/O, exceptions, or state changes.
Abstract away repetitive patterns like error checking.
Monads provide a powerful framework for managing complexity in functional programming while keeping the code expressive and modular.

How Monads Enable Side-Effect Management

One of the key challenges in functional programming is managing side effects—operations that interact with the external world or modify state, such as reading input, writing to files, or generating random numbers. In purely functional languages like Haskell, monads provide a structured way to handle these effects without compromising the principles of immutability and referential transparency.

Key Concepts

Encapsulation of Side Effects
Monads wrap side effects in a controlled context, isolating them from the rest of the program. For example:

The IO monad encapsulates input/output operations.
The State monad manages mutable state.
The Maybe monad handles computations that may fail.

Preservation of Purity

By wrapping side effects in a monadic structure, the core logic remains pure, ensuring that functions produce the same output for the same input. Side effects are deferred and executed only when explicitly needed.

Sequential Composition

Monads provide the >>= (bind) operator, which ensures that side effects are executed in a specific order. This is crucial for maintaining predictable program behavior.

Example: The IO Monad

The IO monad encapsulates input/output operations, such as printing to the console or reading a file.

Code Example:

haskell

Copy code

```
main :: IO ()
main = do
  putStrLn "Enter your name:"
  name <- getLine
  putStrLn ("Hello, " ++ name ++ "!")
```

putStrLn and getLine are IO actions wrapped in the IO monad.

The do notation provides a convenient way to sequence these actions, ensuring they occur in the intended order.

Example: The State Monad

The State monad manages state transitions without mutating global variables.

Code Example:

haskell

Copy code

```haskell
import Control.Monad.State

increment :: State Int Int
increment = do
  n <- get
  put (n + 1)
  return n

result :: (Int, Int)
result = runState increment 10  -- Output: (10, 11)
```

The State monad abstracts state manipulation (reading and updating) into a clean, composable structure.

Benefits of Monads in Side-Effect Management

Modularity: Side-effectful code is separated from pure logic, making the codebase easier to maintain and reason about.
Composability: Monads enable chaining and combining side-effectful operations in a systematic way.
Predictability: Side effects are executed in a well-defined sequence, avoiding unpredictable behavior.
Testability: Core logic remains pure, allowing for easier testing without mocking or simulating side effects.

Conclusion

Monads are the cornerstone of side-effect management in Haskell, allowing functional programs to interact with the real world while maintaining purity and modularity. By encapsulating and sequencing effects, monads provide a robust framework for writing clean, predictable, and maintainable code.

Common Monads in Haskell: Maybe, IO, and List

Monads in Haskell are widely used to manage computations in different contexts, such as handling optional values, side effects, and non-determinism. Three of the most commonly used monads in Haskell are the Maybe, IO, and List monads.

1. The Maybe Monad

The Maybe monad is used to represent computations that might fail or produce no result. It encapsulates an optional value using two constructors:

Just x: Represents a successful computation with the value x.
Nothing: Represents failure or the absence of a value.

Key Features:

Simplifies error handling.

Avoids using explicit condition checks for missing values.

Example:
haskell
Copy code
```
safeDivide :: Int -> Int -> Maybe Int
safeDivide _ 0 = Nothing
safeDivide x y = Just (x `div` y)

result :: Maybe Int
result = Just 10 >>= (\x -> safeDivide x 2) >>= (\y ->
safeDivide y 2)
-- Output: Just 2
```

2. The IO Monad

The IO monad manages input/output operations while keeping them encapsulated within the IO context, preserving purity in functional programming. It allows interaction with the real world, such as reading files, printing to the console, or network communication.

Key Features:

Encapsulates side effects.

Ensures sequential execution of side-effectful operations.

Example:

haskell

Copy code

```
main :: IO ()
main = do
  putStrLn "Enter your name:"
  name <- getLine
  putStrLn ("Hello, " ++ name ++ "!")
```

putStrLn writes to the console, and getLine reads from the user.

The do notation sequences these IO actions.

3. The List Monad

The List monad represents non-deterministic computations, where a computation can return multiple results. Each element of the list represents a possible result.

Key Features:

Allows for operations like filtering and mapping over multiple results.
Used for computations with multiple possibilities, such as searching or combinations.

Example:

haskell
Copy code
```
pairs :: [Int] -> [Int] -> [(Int, Int)]
pairs xs ys = do
  x <- xs
  y <- ys
  return (x, y)

result :: [(Int, Int)]
```

```
result = pairs [1, 2] [3, 4]
-- Output: [(1,3), (1,4), (2,3), (2,4)]
```

Comparison of Maybe, IO, and List Monads

Monad	Purpose	Example Use Cases	
May	Handles Optional values and failure	Safe arithmetic Error Handling	

IO	Encapsulates side effects like I/O	File Handling Console I/O	
List	Determines non deterministic computation	Combinatorial problems, searches.	

Conclusion

These three monads—Maybe, IO, and List—demonstrate the versatility of monads in Haskell. Each addresses a unique computational context while preserving functional purity and modularity, making them essential tools in Haskell programming.

CHAPTER 13
Functional Effects and IO

In functional programming, effects refer to operations that interact with the external world or modify state, such as reading input, writing output, or managing state. Haskell encapsulates these effects using monads, particularly the IO monad, to ensure that side effects are handled in a structured and predictable manner.

Key Features of Functional Effects in IO

Encapsulation

The IO monad wraps side effects, keeping them separate from pure logic. This allows Haskell to maintain referential transparency while enabling real-world interactions.

Sequencing

The IO monad ensures that side-effectful operations are executed in a specific order, using constructs like >>, >>=, and do notation.

Purity Preservation

Side effects are not directly executed but represented as values within the IO monad. Execution happens only when the program is run.

Example: Simple IO in Haskell

haskell

Copy code

```
main :: IO ()
main = do
  putStrLn "What is your name?"
  name <- getLine
  putStrLn ("Hello, " ++ name ++ "!")
```

putStrLn writes to the console, and getLine reads user input.

The do notation sequences these operations.

Functional Effects Beyond IO

Haskell also provides specialized monads to manage other effects, such as:

State: For state management (State monad).
Errors: For error handling (Maybe, Either monads).
Concurrency: For managing concurrent computations (Async, STM monads).

Conclusion

Functional effects in Haskell, particularly through the IO monad, provide a robust framework for handling side effects while preserving functional purity. This makes Haskell a powerful language for writing reliable and maintainable programs that interact with the real world.

Managing Input/Output in Purely Functional Programs

Purely functional programming emphasizes immutability and referential transparency, meaning functions should produce the same output for the same input without causing side effects. Managing input/output (I/O) in such a paradigm can be challenging because I/O inherently involves side effects. In Haskell, this challenge is addressed through the IO monad, which encapsulates I/O operations while maintaining functional purity.

Key Techniques for Managing I/O in Haskell

Encapsulation with the IO Monad

The IO monad wraps side-effectful computations in a controlled manner. This ensures that the rest of the program remains pure, as I/O operations are explicitly marked and isolated.

Example:

haskell

Copy code

```haskell
main :: IO ()
main = do
  putStrLn "What is your name?"
  name <- getLine
  putStrLn ("Hello, " ++ name ++ "!")
```

The IO type in the signature indicates that the function involves side effects.
The do notation sequences these operations.

Deferred Execution

I/O operations are not executed immediately but are instead represented as values of type IO. Execution only occurs when the program is run, preserving the declarative nature of functional programming.

Pure Functions for Processing

While I/O operations are handled in the IO context, the actual processing logic remains pure. This separation improves modularity and testability.

Example:

haskell

Copy code

```
processInput :: String -> String
processInput name = "Hello, " ++ name ++ "!"
```

Combined with I/O:

haskell

Copy code

```
main :: IO ()
main = do
  putStrLn "Enter your name:"
  name <- getLine
  putStrLn (processInput name)
```

Functional Effects for Advanced I/O

Haskell provides libraries like Conduit and Pipes for managing streaming data in a functional way, ensuring that operations remain composable and efficient.

Benefits of Haskell's I/O Approach

Clear Separation of Concerns: I/O and computation are distinctly separated, improving code clarity.
Controlled Side Effects: Encapsulation ensures that side effects do not leak into the pure logic of the program.
Improved Testability: Pure functions are easier to test, as they do not depend on I/O or external state.

Conclusion

Managing I/O in purely functional programs is a challenging but essential aspect of functional programming. Haskell's approach, using the IO monad and separating pure logic from side effects, provides a powerful framework for writing clean, reliable, and maintainable code.

The Role of IO Monad in Haskell

In Haskell, the IO monad plays a crucial role in managing side effects while preserving the language's functional purity. Since purely functional programming relies on immutability and referential transparency, performing input/output (I/O) operations like reading user input, writing to a file, or interacting with the network poses a challenge. The IO monad elegantly addresses this by encapsulating side effects and keeping the rest of the program pure.

What is the IO Monad?

The IO monad is a type constructor in Haskell that represents computations involving side effects. Its primary purpose is to:

Encapsulate Side Effects: Contain and sequence operations that interact with the external world, such as file I/O or console input/output.
Preserve Purity: Isolate impurity within the IO context so that the rest of the program remains pure.
Provide Declarative I/O: Enable I/O operations to be described declaratively rather than imperatively.

How the IO Monad Works

Encapsulation
The IO monad encapsulates actions as values of type IO.

For example:

getLine :: IO String represents an action that reads a string from the user.
putStrLn :: String -> IO () represents an action that writes a string to the console.

Sequencing with do Notation

Haskell uses do notation to sequence IO actions while maintaining a clean and readable syntax. Each action in the sequence runs in order.

Example:

haskell

Copy code

```
main :: IO ()
main = do
  putStrLn "What is your name?"
  name <- getLine
  putStrLn ("Hello, " ++ name ++ "!")
```

The name <- getLine binds the result of the I/O operation to the variable name.

The program remains declarative despite involving side effects.

Deferred Execution

IO actions are not executed immediately. Instead, they are built up as a series of operations within the IO context, and their execution occurs only when the program is run.

Benefits of the IO Monad

Separation of Concerns: Keeps side effects localized, ensuring that other parts of the program remain pure and testable.
Safe I/O Handling: Prevents accidental mixing of pure and impure logic.
Declarative Approach: Allows developers to describe what actions to perform rather than how to perform them.

Example: Reading and Writing to a File

haskell
Copy code
```
import System.IO

main :: IO ()
```

```
main = do
  handle <- openFile "example.txt" ReadMode
  contents <- hGetContents handle
  putStrLn "File contents:"
  putStrLn contents
  hClose handle
```

openFile and hGetContents are IO actions that encapsulate file reading.
The program remains functionally pure outside the IO monad.

Conclusion

The IO monad is fundamental to Haskell's approach to handling side effects. By encapsulating and sequencing impure operations, it allows developers to write real-world applications without sacrificing the benefits of functional programming, such as purity, modularity, and composability.

Building Real-World Applications with IO in Haskell

.

Haskell's IO monad provides the foundation for building real-world applications that interact with the external world while maintaining functional programming principles. Applications like command-line tools, web servers, database interfaces, and file processors can be developed effectively by leveraging Haskell's IO capabilities.

Key Components of Real-World Applications with IO

Console Input/Output

Console-based applications rely heavily on reading input and displaying output. Haskell handles these operations through functions like getLine, putStrLn, and read.

Example:

haskell

Copy code

```
main :: IO ()
main = do
  putStrLn "Enter your name:"
  name <- getLine
  putStrLn ("Hello, " ++ name ++ "!")
```

File Operations

File handling is a common requirement in real-world applications. Haskell provides a set of functions for reading, writing, and managing files, such as openFile, hGetContents, and writeFile.

Example:

haskell

Copy code

```
import System.IO

main :: IO ()
```

```
main = do
  contents <- readFile "example.txt"
  putStrLn "File contents:"
  putStrLn contents
  writeFile "output.txt" ("Modified: " ++ contents)
```

Networking

Networking applications, such as web servers or clients, use libraries like network or http-conduit. The IO monad ensures safe and sequential handling of requests and responses.

Example (using network library):

haskell
Copy code
```
import Network.Socket

main :: IO ()
main = withSocketsDo $ do
  addr <- resolve "127.0.0.1" "3000"
  sock <- openSocket addr
```

```
putStrLn "Listening on port 3000"
listen sock 1
(conn, _) <- accept sock
putStrLn "Connection accepted"
close conn
```

Database Interactions

Libraries like persistent or postgresql-simple allow Haskell programs to perform database operations. These actions are encapsulated within the IO monad to handle connections, queries, and updates.

Concurrency and Parallelism

Real-world applications often require concurrent or parallel processing. Haskell supports this with libraries like async and STM (Software Transactional Memory), enabling safe and efficient concurrent IO operations.

Example (using async):

haskell

Copy code

```
import Control.Concurrent.Async

main :: IO ()
main = do
  a1 <- async (putStrLn "Task 1")
  a2 <- async (putStrLn "Task 2")
  waitBoth a1 a2
```

Best Practices for Building IO-Heavy Applications

Separate Pure and Impure Code

Keep business logic pure and separate from IO operations. This improves testability and modularity.

Use Libraries

Take advantage of Haskell's extensive ecosystem of libraries for file handling, networking, databases, and more.

Handle Errors Gracefully

Use constructs like Maybe, Either, or try from the Control.Exception module to manage errors in IO actions.

Modular Design

Structure the application into small, reusable components to enhance maintainability.

Example: A Simple CLI Calculator

haskell
Copy code
```
import System.IO

calculate :: String -> String
calculate input =
  case words input of
    [x, "+", y] -> show (read x + read y :: Int)
    [x, "-", y] -> show (read x - read y :: Int)
    [x, "*", y] -> show (read x * read y :: Int)
    [x, "/", y] -> show (read x `div` read y :: Int)
```

```
    _        -> "Invalid input"

main :: IO ()
main = do
  putStrLn "Enter a calculation (e.g., 2 + 2):"
  input <- getLine
  putStrLn ("Result: " ++ calculate input)
```

Conclusion

The IO monad empowers developers to build robust, real-world applications in Haskell without compromising on functional programming principles. By effectively separating pure logic from IO operations and utilizing Haskell's powerful libraries and concurrency support, developers can create maintainable and efficient software for a variety of domains.

PART VII: SCALABILITY AND CONCURRENCY IN HASKELL

CHAPTER 14

Scalability with Functional Programming

Functional programming (FP) offers inherent advantages that make it highly suitable for building scalable systems. Its principles—immutability, referential transparency, and declarative design—help manage complexity as systems grow in size and demand.

Key Factors Contributing to Scalability

Immutability

Immutable data structures prevent unexpected state changes, reducing bugs in concurrent and distributed systems. This makes FP ideal for systems that require high concurrency or parallelism.

Stateless Design

Functional programs avoid maintaining internal state, allowing them to scale across distributed architectures like microservices and serverless platforms.

Composability

Small, pure functions can be combined to build complex functionality, promoting modularity and code reuse, which simplifies scaling and maintenance.

Parallelism and Concurrency

FP's immutability ensures thread safety, enabling easier implementation of parallel and concurrent processing, crucial for scaling performance-intensive systems.

Declarative Approach

Functional code expresses what to do rather than how, improving readability and making systems easier to refactor as they scale.

Example: Haskell and Scalability

Haskell's features, such as lazy evaluation, strong typing, and concurrency libraries (e.g., STM and async), make it well-suited for scalable applications.

Example: Scaling a web application with lightweight threads in Haskell:

haskell

Copy code

```
import Control.Concurrent

main :: IO ()
main = do
    mapM_ (\n -> forkIO (putStrLn ("Task " ++ show n)))
[1..100]
```

Conclusion

Functional programming provides a solid foundation for building scalable applications by ensuring robust, modular, and predictable code that handles concurrency and distributed architectures with ease. Its principles simplify scaling, making it an excellent choice for modern software systems.

Building Scalable Systems with Pure Functions

Pure functions are a cornerstone of functional programming, offering a predictable and side-effect-free way to write software. Their deterministic behavior, composability, and thread safety make them particularly well-suited for building scalable systems, especially in environments that require high reliability, modularity, and concurrent processing.

Key Advantages of Pure Functions for Scalability

Predictability

Pure functions always produce the same output for a given input without relying on external state. This makes them easy to test, debug, and scale independently.

Immutability and Thread Safety

Since pure functions do not modify shared state, they are inherently thread-safe. This simplifies parallel and concurrent execution, a critical aspect of scalability.

Composability

Pure functions can be combined to create more complex functionality. This modular design facilitates scaling by allowing individual components to evolve independently.

Statelessness

Pure functions avoid maintaining internal state, enabling horizontal scaling across distributed systems where stateless services can be easily replicated.

Reusability

The isolation and generality of pure functions make them highly reusable, reducing redundancy and enabling scalable codebases.

Applying Pure Functions in Scalable Systems

Data Processing Pipelines

Pure functions are ideal for transforming data in distributed systems, such as MapReduce frameworks or stream processing pipelines.

Example: Transforming a dataset with a pipeline of pure functions in Haskell:

haskell
Copy code
```
processData :: [Int] -> [Int]
processData = map (* 2) . filter (> 10)
```

Concurrent Execution

Functional languages like Haskell or Scala use pure functions to manage concurrency efficiently without risking race conditions or data corruption.
Example: Parallel map in Haskell using the parMap function:

haskell
Copy code
```
import Control.Parallel.Strategies

parallelProcess :: [Int] -> [Int]
parallelProcess xs = parMap rpar (* 2) xs
```

Microservices and Serverless Architectures

Stateless services built with pure functions are easier to deploy and scale in microservices or serverless environments. Each instance operates independently, handling requests without shared dependencies.

Caching and Memoization

Pure functions lend themselves to caching because their outputs depend solely on inputs. This reduces redundant computation in large-scale systems.

Best Practices

Encapsulate Side Effects: Use functional constructs like monads or higher-order functions to isolate side effects, ensuring the core logic remains pure.
Focus on Composition: Design systems as a composition of reusable, pure functions to enable scalability and maintainability.
Leverage Functional Libraries: Use frameworks and libraries that embrace functional principles for concurrent and distributed computing.

Conclusion

Pure functions form the backbone of scalable system design. By ensuring immutability, modularity, and predictable behavior, they simplify the challenges of scaling systems in distributed and parallel environments. Adopting pure functions in your architecture leads to reliable, maintainable, and highly scalable applications.

Managing Large Codebases in Haskell

As software systems grow in complexity, managing large codebases becomes crucial for maintaining readability, scalability, and efficiency. Haskell, with its robust type system, modularity, and functional principles, provides tools and techniques to handle large projects effectively.

Key Strategies for Managing Large Codebases in Haskell

Modular Design

Divide the codebase into smaller, self-contained modules that handle specific functionalities.

Example:

haskell

Copy code

```haskell
-- File: Utils/Math.hs
module Utils.Math (add, subtract) where

add :: Int -> Int -> Int
add x y = x + y

subtract :: Int -> Int -> Int
subtract x y = x - y
```

Each module can be independently developed, tested, and reused.

Type-Driven Development

Leverage Haskell's strong and expressive type system to define clear contracts for functions and data structures.

Use type aliases and newtypes for clarity and to reduce ambiguity in complex projects.

Example:

haskell

Copy code

```
type UserID = Int
newtype Email = Email String
```

Layered Architecture

Organize the code into layers, such as:

Core Logic Layer: Pure functions implementing the main logic.
Infrastructure Layer: Handles side effects like database interactions and file I/O.
API Layer: Exposes functionality to external systems.

Code Formatting and Style

Consistent code style improves readability. Use tools like Ormolu, Fourmolu, or stylish-haskell for formatting.

Documentation and Comments

Write comprehensive documentation using Haddock for modules, functions, and types.
Include inline comments for complex logic.

Error Handling

Use types like Either and Maybe to manage errors explicitly. Libraries like exceptions and safe-exceptions help handle runtime exceptions.
Example:

haskell
Copy code
```
safeDivide :: Int -> Int -> Either String Int
safeDivide _ 0 = Left "Division by zero"
safeDivide x y = Right (x `div` y)
```

Testing and Debugging

Use tools like Hspec and QuickCheck for unit testing and property-based testing.
Debug using GHCi and trace libraries like Debug.Trace.

Dependency Management

Use Cabal or Stack to manage dependencies and build processes.
Pin specific versions of libraries to avoid breaking changes.

Code Reviews and Refactoring

Regularly review code for maintainability. Refactor using type-driven rewrites, ensuring type safety during changes.

Version Control and CI/CD

Use Git for version control, with meaningful commit messages and feature branching.
Automate testing and builds using CI/CD pipelines (e.g., GitHub Actions).

Example: Directory Structure for a Large Haskell Project

bash

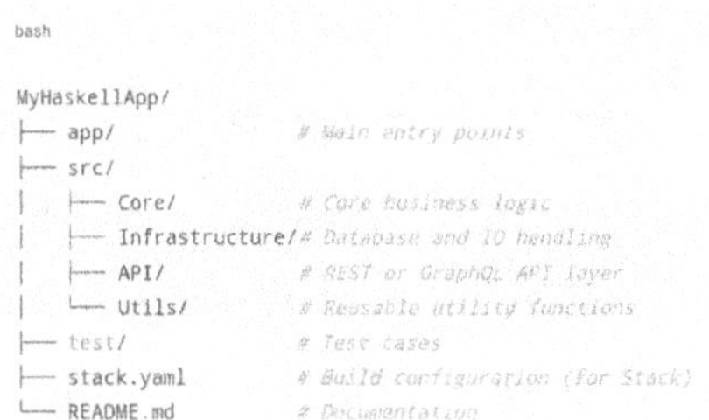

```bash
MyHaskellApp/
├── app/                # Main entry points
├── src/
│   ├── Core/           # Core business logic
│   ├── Infrastructure/# Database and IO handling
│   ├── API/            # REST or GraphQL API layer
│   └── Utils/          # Reusable utility functions
├── test/               # Test cases
├── stack.yaml          # Build configuration (for Stack)
└── README.md           # Documentation
```

Conclusion

Managing large Haskell codebases requires a combination of modular design, type-driven development, and tooling support. By adhering to these best practices, developers can maintain clean, scalable, and maintainable Haskell projects, even as they grow in complexity.

Haskell in Large-Scale Applications

Haskell's unique features—purity, immutability, a strong type system, and advanced abstraction mechanisms—make it well-suited for large-scale applications. While traditionally associated with academic and research contexts, Haskell has gained traction in industries such as fintech, e-commerce, and distributed systems due to its reliability, maintainability, and performance.

Why Use Haskell for Large-Scale Applications?

Reliability Through Strong Typing

Haskell's type system catches many bugs at compile time, reducing runtime errors in production systems. Features like algebraic data types and type classes enable expressive and maintainable code.

Modularity and Reusability

Haskell's functional paradigm promotes modularity through small, pure functions and reusable components. These features simplify managing large codebases.

Concurrency and Parallelism

Haskell excels in handling concurrency and parallelism, making it suitable for applications that demand high performance, such as distributed systems and real-time analytics. Libraries like async, STM (Software Transactional Memory), and GHC's lightweight threads offer powerful tools for concurrency.

Performance Optimization

Haskell's lazy evaluation model enables efficient memory usage, while GHC optimizations ensure competitive performance for computationally intensive applications.

Immutability for Scalability

Immutable data structures eliminate shared mutable state issues, allowing Haskell to scale seamlessly in multi-threaded and distributed environments.

Real-World Applications of Haskell

FinTech and Trading Platforms

Haskell is used in trading systems where correctness and performance are paramount. Companies like Jane Street and Standard Chartered leverage Haskell for complex financial models and risk analysis.

Distributed Systems

Haskell's abstractions simplify the development of distributed applications, offering tools like the Cloud Haskell library for building scalable, fault-tolerant systems.

Web Development

Frameworks like Yesod and Servant enable the creation of robust, type-safe web applications. Haskell's type system ensures API consistency, which is critical for large-scale backend systems.

Compilers and Language Tools

Haskell's syntax and semantics are well-suited for developing compilers and static analysis tools. The language's own compiler, GHC, is a testament to its capabilities.

Machine Learning and Data Analysis

While not as prominent as Python in this field, Haskell libraries like accelerate and hmatrix enable efficient numerical computations for large-scale data processing.

Challenges of Using Haskell at Scale

Steep Learning Curve

Haskell's paradigm differs significantly from imperative programming, requiring developers to invest time in mastering its concepts.

Tooling and Ecosystem

While improving, Haskell's ecosystem may lack the breadth of libraries available in more mainstream languages.

Performance Tuning

Lazy evaluation, while powerful, can introduce subtle performance issues that require expertise to resolve.

Example: Building a Large-Scale Application with Haskell

Use Case: A real-time analytics platform for processing financial transactions.

Features:

High concurrency with STM for transaction safety.

Immutable data pipelines for efficient data transformation.

Type-safe APIs using the Servant framework.

Code Snippet:

haskell

Copy code

```haskell
{-# LANGUAGE DataKinds #-}
{-# LANGUAGE TypeOperators #-}

module Main where

import Control.Concurrent.STM
import Servant

type API = "transactions" :> Get '[JSON] [Transaction]

data Transaction = Transaction
  { txnId :: Int
  , amount :: Double
  } deriving (Show, Eq)

transactions :: TVar [Transaction] -> Handler
[Transaction]
transactions tvar = liftIO $ readTVarIO tvar

server :: TVar [Transaction] -> Server API
```

```
server tvar = transactions tvar

main :: IO ()
main = do
  tvar <- newTVarIO []
  run 8080 $ serve (Proxy :: Proxy API) (server tvar)
```

Conclusion

Haskell is a powerful choice for large-scale applications that require robustness, scalability, and maintainability. Its focus on correctness, coupled with advanced abstractions, makes it well-suited for domains where precision and performance are critical. With proper tools and practices, Haskell can thrive in enterprise-level environments, delivering reliable and efficient systems.

CHAPTER 15
Concurrency and Parallelism in Haskell

Haskell provides powerful abstractions for concurrency and parallelism, enabling efficient multitasking and high-performance computation.

Concurrency: Deals with managing multiple tasks that may interact or block, such as handling multiple client requests. Haskell's lightweight threads (forkIO) and Software Transactional Memory (STM) simplify writing concurrent programs safely and efficiently.

Parallelism: Focuses on executing tasks simultaneously to speed up computations. Haskell supports parallel processing with libraries like parallel and tools like par and pseq for task scheduling across multiple cores.

Key Features:

Lightweight Threads: Thousands of threads managed by the GHC runtime.
STM: Safe and composable state management across threads.
Async Library: High-level abstractions for handling asynchronous tasks.
Haskell's design ensures clear, maintainable, and performant code for concurrent and parallel systems.

The Concept of Concurrency in Functional Programming

Concurrency in functional programming (FP) refers to the ability of a system to handle multiple tasks or processes simultaneously in a way that may involve interleaving their execution. Concurrency focuses on how to structure programs so they can manage multiple tasks, potentially in parallel, while handling issues like blocking, waiting, and coordination between tasks.

Why Concurrency Matters in Functional Programming

Managing Independent Tasks:

In real-world applications, many tasks are independent or only loosely coupled (e.g., handling multiple user requests, performing asynchronous IO operations). Concurrency allows such tasks to run independently without waiting for one another.

Non-blocking Operations:

Concurrency allows the program to continue executing other tasks while waiting for some tasks to complete (e.g., waiting for a network response). In functional programming, this is especially useful for handling IO operations without blocking the main computation.

Handling Shared Resources:

Concurrency helps in managing shared resources safely by ensuring that multiple tasks do not interfere with each other. Functional programming's emphasis on immutability and pure functions makes concurrent programming more straightforward, as data is never modified in place.

Key Concepts in Concurrency for Functional Programming

Immutability and State Management:

Immutability, a core concept in FP, ensures that data is never altered in place. This makes concurrent programming easier because there are no race conditions (where multiple tasks modify the same data simultaneously). Instead, each task works on its own copy of the data.

Pure Functions:

In FP, pure functions have no side effects and always produce the same output for the same input. This makes it easier to reason about concurrent programs because tasks that do not interact with shared mutable state are naturally safer to run concurrently.

Lightweight Threads:

Functional programming languages like Haskell provide abstractions for creating lightweight threads, which are much more efficient than traditional OS-level threads. These threads can run concurrently, with the system managing their execution.

Software Transactional Memory (STM):

STM is a mechanism used to manage state changes across concurrent threads. It enables safe and atomic changes to shared state, making it easier to write correct concurrent programs. In Haskell, STM provides high-level abstractions for handling stateful computations in a concurrent environment.

Asynchronous Programming:

Asynchronous programming allows tasks to execute independently and notify the main program when completed. Functional programming provides abstractions like async and concurrent tasks that allow functions to execute asynchronously without blocking the main computation.

Concurrency in Haskell

Haskell's model of concurrency is built around lightweight threads, immutability, and STM, which makes it an excellent fit for building concurrent systems. Haskell's abstractions, like forkIO for creating threads and STM for managing shared state, allow for building highly concurrent applications with a focus on purity and safety.

Advantages of Concurrency in Functional Programming

Improved Performance: By running multiple tasks concurrently, programs can utilize system resources more efficiently, especially in multi-core environments.

Simplified Reasoning: Since functional programs rely on pure functions and immutable data, developers can reason about concurrent code more easily.
Fault Isolation: Independent tasks can be executed in isolation, reducing the risk of side effects and race conditions.

Conclusion

Concurrency in functional programming allows developers to structure programs to handle multiple tasks simultaneously, efficiently utilizing available resources. In functional languages like Haskell, concurrency is made simpler and safer due to features like immutability, pure functions, and lightweight threads. These features make functional programming especially well-suited for building scalable, responsive, and high-performance systems.

Using Software Transactional Memory (STM) in Haskell

Software Transactional Memory (STM) is a concurrency control mechanism that simplifies managing shared mutable state in concurrent programming. In Haskell, STM is a key feature for handling state in a safe, composable, and efficient manner when working with multiple threads.

STM allows threads to work on shared state without directly modifying it, avoiding race conditions and deadlocks, which are common pitfalls in traditional locking mechanisms.

Key Concepts of STM in Haskell

Transactional Memory:

STM works by wrapping state updates inside transactions, which are composed of a series of operations. A transaction ensures that a set of operations either completes successfully as a whole or doesn't change the state at all (if an error or conflict arises).

TVar (Transactional Variable):

A TVar is the primary building block in STM. It represents a piece of shared state that can be accessed and modified within a transaction. Unlike regular variables, TVars allow updates to be made atomically and isolated from other transactions.

Example:

haskell
Copy code
```
import Control.Concurrent.STM

-- Creating a new transactional variable
counter :: TVar Int
counter = newTVarIO 0  -- Initializes counter to 0
```

Atomic Transactions:

Transactions are executed using the atomically function, which ensures that the changes are committed to the shared state atomically. If a conflict occurs, the transaction is retried automatically until it succeeds.

Example of an atomic transaction:

haskell
Copy code
```
import Control.Concurrent.STM

incrementCounter :: TVar Int -> STM ()
incrementCounter counter = do
  current <- readTVar counter
  writeTVar counter (current + 1)
```

Commit and Rollback:

STM guarantees that either all changes in a transaction are committed to the shared state, or none are, ensuring atomicity. If two threads attempt conflicting transactions (e.g., trying to update the same TVar), one of the transactions is automatically rolled back and retried.

Key STM Functions in Haskell

readTVar:

Reads the current value of a transactional variable.

haskell

Copy code

```
readTVar :: TVar a -> STM a
```

writeTVar:

Writes a new value to a transactional variable.

haskell

Copy code

```
writeTVar :: TVar a -> a -> STM ()
```

atomically:

Executes a transaction, ensuring all operations within it are atomic and isolated.

haskell

Copy code

```
atomically :: STM a -> IO a
```

retry:

If a transaction is in an inconsistent state (e.g., waiting for a condition to become true), it can retry until the condition is met.

haskell
Copy code
```
retry :: STM a
```
orElse:

Allows you to compose alternative transactions, providing a way to try one transaction and, if it fails, retry another.

haskell
Copy code
```
orElse :: STM a -> STM a -> STM a
```

Example: Using STM to Build a Simple Counter

Here's an example of using STM to implement a simple counter with multiple threads incrementing it concurrently:

haskell

Copy code

```
import Control.Concurrent
import Control.Concurrent.STM
import Control.Monad

-- Function to increment the counter
incrementCounter :: TVar Int -> STM ()
incrementCounter counter = do
  current <- readTVar counter
  writeTVar counter (current + 1)

-- Function to print the counter value
printCounter :: TVar Int -> IO ()
printCounter counter = do
  value <- readTVarIO counter
  putStrLn ("Counter value: " ++ show value)
```

```
-- Main function
main :: IO ()
main = do
  counter <- newTVarIO 0  -- Create the counter as a
TVar
 let numThreads = 10

 -- Fork multiple threads that increment the counter
 forM_ [1..numThreads] $ \_ -> do
  forkIO $ atomically $ incrementCounter counter

  -- Wait for threads to complete (simplified for demo
purposes)
 threadDelay 1000000  -- Wait for 1 second

 -- Print the counter value
 printCounter counter
```

In this example, multiple threads concurrently increment the shared counter variable (TVar Int). The use of STM ensures that each update is atomic and consistent, preventing race conditions.

Advantages of STM in Haskell

Safety and Composability:

STM allows safe concurrent programming without the need for locks or other manual synchronization mechanisms. It automatically handles conflicts and retries.

Improved Performance:

STM avoids the performance bottlenecks and complexity of traditional locking mechanisms. In some cases, STM can outperform mutexes or other lock-based approaches, especially in highly concurrent applications.

Easier to Understand:

Since STM abstracts away many of the low-level concurrency details, it allows programmers to reason about concurrent code more easily, without worrying about issues like deadlocks, race conditions, and manual synchronization.

Atomicity:

STM ensures that all changes within a transaction are committed together. If a conflict occurs, the system automatically retries the transaction, maintaining consistency.

Conclusion

Using Software Transactional Memory (STM) in Haskell provides a powerful and declarative way to handle concurrency, simplifying the management of shared state in multi-threaded programs. With STM, Haskell developers can avoid the pitfalls of manual synchronization and concurrency errors, building safer, more maintainable concurrent programs. By leveraging TVars, atomic transactions, and other STM constructs, Haskell provides a high-level and effective way to manage concurrency in functional programming.

Building Concurrent Applications with Haskell

Haskell provides powerful abstractions and libraries for building concurrent applications, enabling developers to write highly parallel, efficient, and scalable programs. Haskell's functional nature, combined with advanced concurrency features like Software Transactional Memory (STM), lightweight threads, and asynchronous I/O, makes it a strong choice for building concurrent applications.

Key Concepts for Concurrency in Haskell

Lightweight Threads: Haskell uses lightweight threads that are managed by the runtime system (RTS), rather than the operating system. This means that thousands or even millions of threads can be created efficiently without incurring significant overhead.

Haskell threads are typically lighter and more scalable than traditional OS threads, making them well-suited for highly concurrent applications such as web servers, simulation systems, and real-time data processing.

Example of creating threads in Haskell:

haskell

Copy code

```
import Control.Concurrent

printMessage :: String -> IO ()
printMessage msg = putStrLn msg

main :: IO ()
main = do
  forkIO $ printMessage "Hello from Thread 1"
  forkIO $ printMessage "Hello from Thread 2"
  threadDelay 1000000  -- Wait for threads to complete
```

In this example, forkIO is used to create lightweight threads that print messages concurrently.

Concurrency with MVar: MVar is a synchronization primitive in Haskell that is commonly used to share state between threads safely. It behaves like a box that can either be empty or contain a value. Threads can take values from or put values into an MVar, ensuring synchronization between them.

Example of using MVar:

haskell
Copy code
```
import Control.Concurrent
import Control.Concurrent.MVar

main :: IO ()
main = do
  mvar <- newEmptyMVar  -- Create an empty MVar
  forkIO $ putMVar mvar "Hello from the other thread"
  message <- takeMVar mvar  -- Take the value from the MVar
  putStrLn message  -- Output the message from the MVar
```

In this example, one thread puts a value into the MVar, while the main thread takes it out and prints it.

Software Transactional Memory (STM): STM in Haskell provides an elegant way to handle shared state in concurrent applications. It allows you to compose transactions that are guaranteed to be atomic, isolating operations on shared variables from the rest of the program.

Example of using STM for concurrency:

haskell

Copy code

```
import Control.Concurrent.STM

incrementCounter :: TVar Int -> STM ()
incrementCounter counter = do
  current <- readTVar counter
  writeTVar counter (current + 1)

main :: IO ()
main = do
   counter <- newTVarIO 0  -- Initialize a transactional
variable
```

```
forkIO $ atomically $ incrementCounter counter
forkIO $ atomically $ incrementCounter counter
threadDelay 1000000  -- Wait for threads to complete
value <- readTVarIO counter
putStrLn $ "Final counter value: " ++ show value
```

STM provides a way to compose safe concurrent transactions using TVar variables and atomically to ensure consistency even when multiple threads are involved.

Asynchronous I/O: Haskell's asynchronous I/O libraries, such as async and concurrent (from the Control.Concurrent.Async module), provide the ability to perform I/O operations concurrently without blocking the main program.

Example of asynchronous I/O:

haskell

Copy code

```
import Control.Concurrent.Async
```

```
main :: IO ()
main = do
  asyncTask1 <- async (putStrLn "Task 1 is running")
  asyncTask2 <- async (putStrLn "Task 2 is running")
  wait asyncTask1
  wait asyncTask2
```

The async function allows you to run tasks concurrently and the wait function waits for the result of each task, allowing your application to perform multiple I/O operations in parallel.

Patterns for Building Concurrent Applications

Producer-Consumer Model: This pattern is often used when one or more threads (producers) generate data that needs to be consumed by other threads (consumers). Using concurrency primitives like MVar or TVar allows safe sharing of data between threads.

Example:

haskell

Copy code

```
import Control.Concurrent
import Control.Concurrent.MVar

producer :: MVar String -> IO ()
producer mvar = do
  putMVar mvar "Data produced"
  threadDelay 1000000  -- Simulate work

consumer :: MVar String -> IO ()
consumer mvar = do
  dataConsumed <- takeMVar mvar
  putStrLn $ "Consumed: " ++ dataConsumed

main :: IO ()
main = do
  mvar <- newEmptyMVar
  forkIO $ producer mvar
  forkIO $ consumer mvar

  threadDelay 2000000  -- Wait for threads to complete
```

In this example, the producer creates data and puts it into an MVar, and the consumer takes the data from the MVar and processes it.

Map-Reduce: The Map-Reduce pattern is useful for processing large datasets by dividing the work into smaller tasks. Haskell's concurrency tools make it easy to parallelize these tasks.

Example (map-reduce pattern):

haskell
Copy code
```
import Control.Concurrent
import Control.Concurrent.Async

-- Simulate a map operation
mapOperation :: Int -> Int
mapOperation x = x * 2

-- Reduce function (summing the results)
reduce :: [Int] -> Int
reduce = sum
```

```
main :: IO ()
main = do
  let dataToProcess = [1, 2, 3, 4, 5]
   asyncResults <- mapM (async . return . mapOperation)
dataToProcess
  results <- mapM wait asyncResults
  let finalResult = reduce results
  putStrLn $ "Final result: " ++ show finalResult
```

In this example, the map function is applied to each element concurrently, and then the reduce function is used to combine the results.

Advantages of Concurrency in Haskell

Lightweight Threads:

Haskell provides a high degree of concurrency through lightweight threads, which allows for scalable and efficient handling of large numbers of tasks or connections.

Composability:

Concurrency primitives like STM and MVar allow for building composable, modular concurrent applications. Haskell's functional nature makes it easier to compose complex concurrent behaviors.

Simpler Error Handling:

Because Haskell handles concurrency at a higher level, developers can avoid many of the issues associated with manual thread management, like deadlocks or race conditions. The runtime system automatically handles scheduling, and STM ensures atomicity of transactions.

Performance:

Haskell's concurrency model is highly optimized, and when combined with STM and lazy evaluation, it can perform well even in highly concurrent environments. Haskell's RTS also ensures efficient thread scheduling, which reduces overhead.

Conclusion

Building concurrent applications in Haskell involves leveraging lightweight threads, STM, and asynchronous I/O to write scalable, efficient, and safe programs. By combining Haskell's powerful concurrency primitives with its functional programming paradigm, developers can manage state, handle multiple threads, and perform tasks concurrently while maintaining a clean, composable codebase. Whether building web servers, real-time systems, or distributed applications, Haskell's concurrency model provides the tools to handle complexity in a declarative and efficient manner.

PART VIII: ADVANCED TOPICS AND REAL-WORLD APPLICATIONS

CHAPTER 16

Building Libraries and Frameworks in Haskell

Building libraries and frameworks in Haskell involves creating reusable, modular, and maintainable software components that can be shared across multiple projects. Haskell's strong type system, immutability, and pure functional programming model make it well-suited for creating high-quality libraries and frameworks.

Modularity: Break down functionality into small, composable functions that can be easily reused. Haskell's type system ensures correctness and clarity in APIs.

Type Classes: Leverage type classes for generic programming, enabling code to work with multiple data types while maintaining safety and flexibility.

Error Handling: Use Maybe, Either, or custom error types instead of exceptions for predictable and safe error handling.

Extensibility: Frameworks should be designed to be easily extended through Haskell's powerful abstractions, such as higher-order functions and type classes.

Integration with Other Libraries: Seamlessly integrate with other libraries and tools, allowing for efficient development of complex applications.

Concurrency: Use Haskell's lightweight threads, STM (Software Transactional Memory), and other concurrency tools to build scalable, concurrent applications.

In Haskell, libraries and frameworks can be packaged and distributed using Cabal, Haskell's package manager, and documented with Haddock. Haskell's focus on immutability, type safety, and functional programming makes it an excellent choice for building reliable and reusable software components.

Design Principles for Haskell Libraries

When designing Haskell libraries, it is important to follow certain principles to ensure that the library is efficient, maintainable, extensible, and usable. The functional nature of Haskell, along with its strong type system, enables the creation of robust and reusable software components. Here are some key design principles for Haskell libraries:

Modularity and Reusability:

Small and Focused Functions: Design functions that perform one task well, following the Unix philosophy of "doing one thing and doing it well." This makes your library easier to maintain and test.

Separation of Concerns: Break down complex functionality into smaller, composable modules. Each module should have a clear responsibility, making it easier for others to use and understand.

Pure Functions: Leverage pure functions that don't have side effects. This ensures referential transparency and makes your library predictable and easier to reason about.

Type Safety:

Strong Type System: Utilize Haskell's type system to enforce correctness. Use algebraic data types, type classes, and type inference to catch errors at compile time.

Minimize Use of Any: Avoid the use of overly general types (like Any) unless necessary, as they reduce the safety and clarity of your library's API.

Immutability:

Prefer Immutable Data: Immutability should be the default. Avoid mutable state, which can introduce bugs and makes code harder to test and reason about.
Design for Immutability: Create libraries that work efficiently with immutable data structures, and ensure that any changes to data are done through transformations (e.g., using map, fold, etc.).

Error Handling:

Use Maybe and Either: For functions that might fail, use Maybe for simple failure (e.g., Nothing) or Either for more detailed error handling. This allows users of your library to handle errors explicitly.
Avoid Exceptions: Try to minimize the use of exceptions as they break referential transparency and can lead to side effects. Use algebraic data types for predictable error handling instead.

Abstraction and Generalization:

Type Classes for Polymorphism: Use type classes to define common behaviors across different types. This allows for flexibility while maintaining type safety and ensures your library can work with a wide variety of data types.

Generic Functions: Build generic functions that can operate on a wide range of types without duplicating code. Haskell's type classes and higher-kinded types allow you to abstract common functionality.

Documentation and Usability:

Clear API Design: Ensure that your library's API is easy to understand and intuitive. A well-designed API should be easy to use, with minimal learning curve.

Comprehensive Documentation: Provide thorough documentation, including examples and explanations of key concepts. Use tools like Haddock to generate documentation from your source code.

Minimal Dependencies: Keep dependencies to a minimum, as excessive dependencies can introduce complexity and reduce the portability of your library.

Performance:

Efficient Use of Data Structures: Choose the appropriate data structures for your library's use cases. Haskell has a rich set of immutable data structures, and using the right one can significantly affect performance.
Lazy Evaluation: Make good use of Haskell's lazy evaluation for performance optimizations. However, be mindful of the potential pitfalls of laziness, such as increased memory usage or performance bottlenecks.
Avoid Space Leaks: Design your library to avoid space leaks by carefully managing memory, especially when working with lazy data structures or IO operations.

Testing and Quality:

Unit Testing: Write unit tests to verify that your functions behave as expected. Haskell's rich type system and purity make it easier to write tests, as functions are more predictable and side effects are limited.
Property-Based Testing: Use property-based testing frameworks like QuickCheck to verify that your library's functions behave correctly under a wide range of conditions. This is especially useful for higher-order functions and algorithms that operate on generic types.

Compatibility and Versioning:

Backward Compatibility: When updating your library, ensure that changes are backward compatible, or clearly document breaking changes. Semver (semantic versioning) can help with managing version numbers and dependencies.
Cross-Platform Support: Consider the environment where your library will be used (e.g., GHC versions, operating systems). Ensure that your library works across various platforms where it might be deployed.

By following these design principles, you can create Haskell libraries that are efficient, maintainable, and flexible, while ensuring they integrate smoothly with the Haskell ecosystem.

Testing and Debugging Haskell Code

Testing and debugging are essential practices in software development, and Haskell provides powerful tools and methodologies to ensure the correctness, reliability, and maintainability of your code. Given Haskell's functional nature, immutability, and strong type system, these practices are streamlined, though they come with unique challenges. Here's a guide to testing and debugging in Haskell:

1. Unit Testing in Haskell

Unit testing involves verifying that individual components of your code (functions, modules) work as expected. Haskell provides several tools and libraries to make unit testing easier:

HUnit: A widely used unit testing library for Haskell. It provides basic assertion functionality to check that your functions return the expected results.

haskell
Copy code
```
import Test.HUnit

-- Sample function
add :: Int -> Int -> Int
add x y = x + y

-- Unit test for the add function
testAdd = TestCase (assertEqual "for add 1 + 2" 3 (add 1 2))

main :: IO Counts
main = runTestTT testAdd
```

QuickCheck: A property-based testing tool, which allows you to write properties (conditions that must always hold) and then generates test cases to check if the properties hold for random inputs. It's especially useful for testing functions that operate on generic types or complex data structures.

haskell
Copy code
```
import Test.QuickCheck

-- Property: adding zero to any number should return the number
prop_addZero :: Int -> Bool
prop_addZero x = add x 0 == x

main = quickCheck prop_addZero
```

Tasty: A testing framework that integrates with various testing libraries (like HUnit and QuickCheck). It helps in running tests and generating reports.

haskell
Copy code

```
import Test.Tasty
import Test.Tasty.HUnit

testAdd = testCase "1 + 2 equals 3" (add 1 2 @?= 3)

main :: IO ()
main = defaultMain $ testGroup "Tests" [testAdd]
```

2. Property-Based Testing

Property-based testing goes beyond checking for fixed values and tests whether certain properties always hold, given a wide variety of inputs. It is a hallmark of functional programming and is essential for testing functions that must handle a broad range of cases.

Properties to Check: For instance, when testing a sorting function, a property might be that the result is always sorted, or when adding two numbers, the result is always greater than or equal to both numbers.

QuickCheck can generate random input values and run your properties automatically, making it easier to catch edge cases and subtle bugs.

haskell

Copy code

```
import Test.QuickCheck

-- Property: Sorting a list results in a sorted list
prop_sorted :: [Int] -> Bool
prop_sorted xs = sorted (sort xs)
  where
    sorted [] = True
    sorted [x] = True
    sorted (x:y:xs) = x <= y && sorted (y:xs)

main = quickCheck prop_sorted
```

3. Debugging Haskell Code

Debugging in Haskell can be challenging due to its immutability, laziness, and functional style. However, there are several tools and techniques that can help identify and resolve issues effectively.

GHCi (Glasgow Haskell Compiler Interactive): GHCi is a REPL (Read-Eval-Print Loop) that allows you to interactively load and test parts of your program. It's helpful for experimenting with code, inspecting variables, and debugging functions.

Loading your code:

bash
Copy code
```
ghci MyModule.hs
```

Inspecting functions: You can evaluate functions in GHCi and inspect their results:

haskell
Copy code
```
*Main> add 1 2
```

3

trace function: The Debug.Trace module provides the trace function, which allows you to insert debugging output into your code. This can be useful for tracing function calls and values without needing to modify the overall structure of your code.

haskell
Copy code
```
import Debug.Trace

add x y = trace ("Adding " ++ show x ++ " and " ++ show y) (x + y)
```

The trace function logs messages while allowing the program to continue execution. However, be cautious, as this is a side-effecting operation, and using it excessively can lead to side effects that go against Haskell's functional paradigm.

Haskell Debugger (GHC Debugger - GDB): You can use GDB (GNU Debugger) with Haskell programs compiled with GHC to set breakpoints and inspect code execution step by step. This method is useful for more intricate debugging and performance analysis.

4. Testing and Debugging in Parallel/Concurrent Code

When working with concurrent or parallel programs in Haskell, debugging becomes more complex due to the non-deterministic nature of thread execution. Some strategies for debugging parallel/concurrent Haskell code include:

Use of Control.Concurrent.Debug: Haskell provides debugging support for concurrent code via the Control.Concurrent.Debug module. This module allows you to trace and monitor the behavior of threads during execution.

Software Transactional Memory (STM): When working with STM in Haskell, you can debug the transactional behaviors of your program. STM's composability and isolation properties can help avoid certain classes of concurrency bugs.

Use of debug flag: To debug concurrency issues, you can compile the program with debugging flags and check thread behaviors in GHC's output.

5. Common Challenges and Debugging Tips

Lazy Evaluation: Because of lazy evaluation, a common bug in Haskell can be unexpected memory usage or non-termination. It's important to ensure that lazy data structures are evaluated when needed, especially in performance-critical code.

Use strict versions of functions (e.g., seq, deepseq) to evaluate data structures eagerly when needed.
Space Leaks: A space leak happens when a program holds onto memory it no longer needs. To diagnose space leaks, you can use the +RTS -s flag to get a memory usage summary or use profiling tools like GHC Profiler.

Concurrency Issues: When dealing with concurrency, issues such as deadlocks and race conditions can arise.

These can often be mitigated by leveraging higher-level concurrency abstractions like MVar, STM, or async.

6. Best Practices for Testing and Debugging in Haskell

Write Tests First: Practice Test-Driven Development (TDD) to write tests before implementing functionality. This helps ensure that your code is testable and that it behaves as expected.

Use Functional Patterns: Use declarative and functional patterns in your code to make it more predictable and easier to test.

Modular Design: Write modular and composable functions that can be independently tested and reasoned about.

Leverage Haskell's Type System: The type system can help catch many errors at compile time, reducing the need for debugging later.

By following these principles and utilizing Haskell's robust testing and debugging tools, you can ensure the correctness and reliability of your programs while keeping your development process efficient and maintainable.

Using Haskell for Domain-Specific Languages (DSLs)

Domain-Specific Languages (DSLs) are custom programming languages designed for specific problem domains, offering tailored syntax and functionality to express solutions in a more concise and intuitive manner. Haskell, with its powerful type system, higher-order functions, and abstraction capabilities, is particularly well-suited for designing and implementing DSLs. Here's a guide to using Haskell for creating DSLs:

1. Why Use Haskell for DSLs?

Haskell's functional nature makes it an excellent choice for designing DSLs, as it allows you to create elegant, composable, and reusable language constructs. Some key reasons why Haskell is ideal for DSL development are:

Strong Type System: Haskell's advanced type system ensures that the DSL can be safe and expressive. It can enforce constraints, ensure correctness, and provide rich error messages at compile time.

Higher-Order Functions: Haskell's support for higher-order functions allows you to abstract over the constructs of the DSL and compose them efficiently.

Purity and Immutability: Haskell's emphasis on immutability and pure functions makes DSLs more predictable and easier to reason about.

Flexible Syntax: Haskell provides mechanisms to create custom syntax via libraries and extensions, making it easy to implement a domain-specific language that is both expressive and user-friendly.

2. Types of DSLs in Haskell

DSLs can be broadly categorized into two types:

Internal DSLs: These are DSLs embedded within a host language (in this case, Haskell). Internal DSLs allow you to write domain-specific code using the host language's syntax, extended to provide domain-specific functionality.

External DSLs: These DSLs have their own syntax and grammar, and the host language (Haskell) is responsible for parsing, interpreting, or compiling the DSL code into executable code.

Haskell is most commonly used to create internal DSLs, where the domain-specific code is written using Haskell's syntax but tailored for the domain.

3. Building Internal DSLs in Haskell

An internal DSL is essentially a set of functions, data types, and combinators in Haskell that give the appearance of a specialized language. It uses the host language's syntax but can present a more readable and expressive interface for specific tasks.

Example: A Simple Arithmetic DSL

Let's create a simple DSL for arithmetic expressions:

haskell
Copy code
```
-- Define a basic type for expressions
data Expr = Const Int
          | Add Expr Expr
          | Multiply Expr Expr
          deriving (Show)

-- Evaluate the expression
eval :: Expr -> Int
eval (Const n) = n
eval (Add x y) = eval x + eval y
eval (Multiply x y) = eval x * eval y
```

```
-- Example usage of the DSL
expr1 = Add (Const 5) (Multiply (Const 2) (Const 3))
```

In this case, the syntax is Haskell code, but it represents a simple arithmetic expression in a domain-specific manner. The use of Add and Multiply creates a more natural representation of an arithmetic expression.

Combinators for Domain-Specific Behavior

To create a more advanced internal DSL, you can define combinators, functions that operate on the domain objects to create more complex constructs.

haskell

Copy code

```
-- A combinator that creates an expression for subtraction
subtractExpr :: Expr -> Expr -> Expr
subtractExpr x y = Add x (Multiply (Const (-1)) y)

-- A combinator for exponentiation
```

```haskell
expExpr :: Expr -> Expr -> Expr
expExpr base exp = Multiply base (Const 2) -- Simplified example for illustration
```

The combination of these combinators lets you create more complex domain-specific functionality while maintaining a high level of abstraction.

4. Building External DSLs in Haskell

An external DSL has its own syntax, and building one in Haskell typically involves parsing and interpreting the DSL code. Haskell's libraries for parsing and lexing, such as Parsec, Attoparsec, and Happy, are commonly used for creating external DSLs.

Example: A Simple DSL Parser
Let's define a simple external DSL for arithmetic expressions:

haskell
Copy code

```haskell
import Text.Parsec
```

```
import Text.Parsec.String (Parser)

-- Define the arithmetic grammar
expr :: Parser Expr
expr = try addExpr <|> try multiplyExpr <|> constExpr

addExpr :: Parser Expr
addExpr = do
 x <- constExpr
 _ <- char '+'
 y <- constExpr
 return (Add x y)

multiplyExpr :: Parser Expr
multiplyExpr = do
 x <- constExpr
 _ <- char '*'
 y <- constExpr
 return (Multiply x y)

constExpr :: Parser Expr
constExpr = do
 n <- many1 digit
```

```
return (Const (read n))

-- Example usage: parse an expression string
parseExpr :: String -> Either ParseError Expr
parseExpr input = parse expr "" input
```

In this example, we use the Parsec library to define a simple arithmetic DSL that can parse expressions like 3 + 4 or 5 * 6. We start by defining a parser for basic arithmetic expressions, and then combine them into a more complex one.

5. Using Libraries for DSLs in Haskell

To make DSL development easier, Haskell provides several libraries:

Domain-Specific Libraries (DSLs): Haskell has libraries such as DSL and haskell-src that offer utilities for building and manipulating DSLs.

Parser Combinator Libraries: Libraries like Parsec and Attoparsec are essential when building external DSLs.

They allow you to define complex grammars and parse DSL syntax into data structures.

Hakyll: A popular Haskell library for creating static websites, which itself is a DSL for building websites. Hakyll demonstrates how DSLs can be used to describe the structure and layout of websites.

Lens and Optics: These libraries allow you to define lenses, prisms, and other compositional abstractions that can be used to manipulate complex data structures in a concise manner, making them useful in DSLs for managing and transforming state.

6. Advantages of Using Haskell for DSLs

Type Safety: Haskell's strong and expressive type system provides static guarantees about the correctness of the DSL code, reducing runtime errors.

Concise and Expressive Syntax: With higher-order functions and function composition, Haskell allows you to build a DSL with a natural and concise syntax.

Extensibility: You can easily extend an internal DSL by adding new combinators, functions, and features, all while keeping the DSL code readable and maintainable.

Performance: Haskell is a highly performant language, making it possible to create efficient DSL implementations that can handle large-scale applications.

7. Challenges of Using Haskell for DSLs

Learning Curve: For developers not familiar with Haskell, building DSLs can involve a steep learning curve, especially when working with complex type systems or advanced functional patterns.

Complexity: While Haskell's features provide significant power, they can also lead to complex code, which may be difficult to maintain if not carefully structured.

Integration with Other Tools: Integrating Haskell-based DSLs with other parts of a system (written in other languages) may require additional effort for interoperation or embedding.

8. Conclusion

Haskell is an excellent choice for building Domain-Specific Languages, whether you need an internal DSL for expressing domain logic concisely within a larger application, or an external DSL for creating a standalone language with custom syntax. Its advanced type system, higher-order functions, and powerful abstraction tools enable the creation of highly expressive and maintainable DSLs, making it a powerful tool for developers looking to solve domain-specific problems efficiently.

CHAPTER 17
Haskell in Web and Distributed Systems

Haskell is a robust choice for building web and distributed systems due to its strong type system, immutability, and concurrency features. These characteristics make it ideal for applications requiring reliability, scalability, and maintainability.

Web Development:

Haskell frameworks like Yesod, Spock, and Scotty enable the development of secure and high-performance web applications. They provide type-safe routing, templating, and form handling, minimizing runtime errors.

APIs and Microservices:

Haskell's concise syntax and strong typing ensure robust API development. Libraries like Servant allow you to define APIs in a type-safe way, ensuring that documentation, implementation, and client generation are consistent.

Concurrency for Distributed Systems:

Haskell excels in managing concurrency with abstractions like STM (Software Transactional Memory) and lightweight threads. Libraries such as distributed-process support building fault-tolerant, scalable distributed systems.

Reliability and Safety:

Functional programming principles in Haskell lead to predictable and maintainable systems, reducing bugs and improving security—a critical requirement for web and distributed systems.

Challenges:

While Haskell provides powerful tools, the learning curve and limited ecosystem compared to mainstream web technologies may require additional effort for adoption and integration.

Haskell's strengths make it an excellent choice for web and distributed systems where correctness, performance, and scalability are priorities.

Functional Web Development with Haskell

Functional web development with Haskell leverages its strong type system, immutability, and declarative programming model to build robust, maintainable, and scalable web applications. Haskell's features make it particularly suited for ensuring correctness, reducing bugs, and simplifying complex workflows in web development.

Key Aspects of Functional Web Development in Haskell:
Type-Safe Frameworks:

Haskell web frameworks like Yesod, Spock, and Scotty offer type-safe solutions for routing, request handling, and response generation. These frameworks reduce runtime errors by catching issues at compile time.

Declarative APIs:

Libraries such as Servant enable you to define APIs declaratively. The API specifications double as documentation, server implementation, and client generation, ensuring consistency across the system.

Purely Functional Programming:

Haskell's functional nature promotes predictable, side-effect-free code, leading to easier debugging and testing. State management becomes straightforward with immutability and functional paradigms.

Concurrency and Parallelism:

Concurrency is crucial for web applications, and Haskell's lightweight threads and STM (Software Transactional Memory) make it easy to handle multiple requests efficiently. These features are ideal for real-time and high-throughput systems.

Templating and Content Rendering:

Haskell offers templating engines like Blaze and Heist, which integrate seamlessly into functional workflows. These tools allow dynamic and type-safe HTML generation.

Static Analysis and Security:

The strong typing and immutability in Haskell reduce vulnerabilities, ensuring safer code for handling user inputs and preventing common attacks such as injection flaws.

Challenges:

Functional web development in Haskell can have a steep learning curve, especially for developers unfamiliar with functional programming. The ecosystem, while powerful, is smaller compared to mainstream web technologies.

Benefits:

Reduced runtime errors due to strong type checking.
Easier debugging and testing through pure functions.
Improved scalability and performance with advanced concurrency models.

Haskell provides a modern and reliable approach to web development for projects where correctness, maintainability, and performance are paramount.

Building Distributed Systems with Haskell

Haskell's functional programming paradigm, strong type system, and powerful concurrency tools make it an ideal language for building distributed systems. With its focus on immutability, referential transparency, and high-level abstractions for managing concurrency and parallelism, Haskell helps developers build scalable, reliable, and fault-tolerant distributed systems.

Key Aspects of Building Distributed Systems with Haskell:

Concurrency and Parallelism:

Haskell's lightweight threads, software transactional memory (STM), and advanced concurrency primitives are particularly suited for handling the complex and highly concurrent nature of distributed systems. Haskell's Concurrency Model allows handling thousands of tasks concurrently, which is essential in distributed environments where tasks need to run in parallel across multiple machines.

Fault Tolerance:

Distributed systems need to be resilient to failures. Haskell's monads (such as the IO Monad) allow for the encapsulation of side effects in a controlled manner, which simplifies the creation of fault-tolerant systems. Libraries like distributed-process enable actors and message-passing models, making it easier to build systems that can recover from failures.

Scalability:

.

The immutability and statelessness of Haskell's functional programming model align well with distributed systems, where scalability is crucial. Haskell's pure functions and powerful abstractions for managing state enable easier distribution of tasks across multiple nodes in a cluster. Tools like Cloud Haskell allow Haskell programs to be distributed across multiple machines while ensuring that the logic remains consistent.

Network Communication:

Building a distributed system requires efficient and secure communication between different components. Haskell's libraries like network and pipes provide abstractions for building scalable networked applications that can easily handle message passing and data exchange between components in distributed systems.

Software Transactional Memory (STM):

Haskell's STM is a crucial tool for managing shared mutable state in distributed systems. STM helps manage consistency across distributed systems by providing a high-level interface for managing state updates without the need for complex locking mechanisms, ensuring that the system remains safe and deadlock-free.

Distributed Systems Libraries:

Haskell provides several specialized libraries for distributed systems, such as Cloud Haskell and Network-Transport, which facilitate building systems where components can be distributed across different machines or nodes. These libraries abstract the complexities of network communication and error handling, allowing developers to focus on business logic.

Real-Time and Event-Driven Systems:

Haskell's ability to handle asynchronous I/O operations efficiently with lightweight threads makes it well-suited for real-time and event-driven systems, which are common in distributed applications like messaging platforms, live data processing, or financial systems.

Consistency and CAP Theorem:

Distributed systems face the challenge of maintaining consistency while ensuring availability and partition tolerance (CAP theorem). Haskell provides tools that support designing systems that can handle these trade-offs efficiently, such as eventual consistency models or strongly consistent systems with the help of libraries like replica and zookeeper.

Benefits:

High-Level Abstractions: Haskell's functional paradigm allows developers to abstract away many of the complexities of distributed system design, such as managing state or handling side effects.
Concurrency: With lightweight threads and STM, Haskell is particularly strong in managing concurrency, which is essential in distributed systems.
Immutability and Fault Tolerance: Haskell's immutability makes it easier to handle distributed state changes and recover from failures.

Challenges:

Learning Curve: While Haskell offers many advantages, it has a steep learning curve, especially for developers coming from an imperative programming background.
Ecosystem Size: The ecosystem for distributed systems in Haskell is smaller compared to other mainstream languages like Java or Python, meaning that fewer out-of-the-box solutions may be available.

In summary, Haskell provides a powerful, reliable, and scalable foundation for building distributed systems. With its high-level abstractions, robust concurrency support, and ability to manage state and side effects, Haskell enables the development of complex distributed applications that are both efficient and resilient to failure.

Haskell in the Cloud

Haskell is increasingly being used for cloud computing applications due to its strengths in concurrency, type safety, and functional programming. The cloud provides a scalable infrastructure for Haskell-based applications, allowing developers to leverage its capabilities for building robust, maintainable, and high-performance solutions.

Key Features of Haskell for Cloud Computing:

Concurrency and Scalability:

Haskell's lightweight threads and concurrency libraries, such as async and STM, make it an excellent choice for building scalable applications in the cloud. These features enable efficient handling of concurrent requests and tasks, which are common in cloud environments.

Type Safety and Reliability:

Haskell's strong type system ensures that code is robust and error-free, which is critical for cloud applications that require high reliability. Type safety reduces runtime errors, making cloud deployments more stable.

Stateless and Serverless Computing:

Functional programming principles in Haskell align well with stateless and serverless computing models. Haskell functions can easily be deployed as serverless components, such as AWS Lambda functions, for handling specific tasks in a cloud-native way.

Microservices Architecture:

Haskell's modularity and composability make it suitable for building microservices. Frameworks like Servant allow developers to create type-safe APIs, ensuring consistent and error-free communication between services.

Cloud Libraries and Frameworks:

Haskell has libraries for integrating with popular cloud platforms:

AWS: Libraries like amazonka provide tools for interacting with AWS services such as S3, EC2, and DynamoDB.
Google Cloud: Haskell libraries and REST clients can interact with Google Cloud APIs for services like BigQuery and Cloud Storage.

Azure: REST-based integrations allow Haskell to interact with Microsoft Azure's cloud offerings.

Distributed Systems:

Haskell's support for distributed computing with libraries like Cloud Haskell enables developers to build scalable systems that can run across multiple nodes in a cloud environment. This is ideal for applications requiring fault tolerance and horizontal scaling.

Infrastructure as Code (IaC):

Haskell can be used to define and manage cloud infrastructure programmatically. Tools like dhall and Haskell-based scripting capabilities allow developers to write reproducible, type-checked infrastructure configurations.

Real-Time Data Processing:

Haskell's efficiency in handling streams of data makes it suitable for real-time processing in the cloud. Libraries like conduit and pipes can be combined with cloud-based event-driven architectures to handle massive streams of data effectively.

Benefits:

Performance: Haskell's laziness and strong typing lead to efficient cloud applications that minimize resource usage.
Safety: Type checking and immutability ensure that cloud systems are less prone to bugs, making deployments safer.
Cost Efficiency: Haskell's efficiency in handling concurrent processes can reduce cloud infrastructure costs by optimizing resource utilization.

Challenges:

Learning Curve: Haskell's advanced concepts can be challenging for newcomers, potentially slowing down cloud project development.

Limited Ecosystem: Compared to more widely used languages like Python or Java, Haskell's cloud ecosystem is smaller, requiring more custom development.

Haskell's functional paradigm and strong concurrency support make it a powerful tool for cloud computing. Its capabilities align well with the demands of cloud-native applications, from microservices to real-time data processing, offering a unique blend of performance, reliability, and maintainability.

CHAPTER 18
Advanced Patterns and Best Practices

Haskell offers a range of advanced programming patterns and best practices that allow developers to write clean, efficient, and maintainable code. Mastering these patterns is essential for tackling complex projects and leveraging the full potential of the language.

Key Advanced Patterns:

Monadic Design:

Monads, such as Maybe, Either, and IO, are foundational in Haskell for managing side effects, errors, and computations. Understanding how to chain monadic operations effectively leads to cleaner, more composable code.

Applicative Functors:

Applicatives are a generalization of monads, allowing computations to be combined independently. They are especially useful for scenarios like validating multiple inputs simultaneously.

Functional Reactive Programming (FRP):

FRP enables managing complex event-driven systems, such as GUIs or real-time data streams, using abstractions like behaviors and events.

Higher-Kinded Types:

These allow the creation of highly abstract and reusable components, enabling developers to write generic code that works across various data types and structures.

Lens Library:

The lens library simplifies working with deeply nested data structures by providing composable and reusable ways to access and modify data.

Best Practices:

Embrace Type Safety:

Leverage Haskell's type system to enforce invariants, document code behavior, and catch errors at compile time.

Pure Functions:

Write pure, side-effect-free functions wherever possible. This simplifies reasoning about code and improves testability.

Avoid Overusing IO:

Minimize the scope of IO to keep the codebase more modular and testable. Use monads like Reader or State to manage effects without resorting to IO.

Use Abstractions Wisely:

Balance abstraction with readability. Advanced features like monads and lenses are powerful but can make the code harder to understand for newcomers.

Optimize for Performance:

Use profiling tools and understand lazy evaluation to avoid common performance pitfalls like space leaks.

By mastering these advanced patterns and adhering to best practices, Haskell developers can build robust, scalable, and elegant software that leverages the full power of functional programming.

Functors, Applicatives, and Other Abstract Concepts

Haskell's type classes such as Functor, Applicative, and others provide a framework for abstracting over common patterns of computation. These abstractions allow developers to write reusable and composable code.

1. Functors

A Functor represents a type that can be mapped over. It provides the fmap function to apply a function to the values inside a container without altering the structure of the container.

Definition:

haskell

Copy code

```
class Functor f where
  fmap :: (a -> b) -> f a -> f b
```

Example:

haskell

Copy code

```
fmap (+1) (Just 2) -- Result: Just 3
fmap (*2) [1, 2, 3] -- Result: [2, 4, 6]
```

2. Applicatives

Applicative extends Functor by allowing the application of functions that are themselves within a context (e.g., Maybe, [], etc.).

Definition:

haskell

Copy code

```
class Functor f => Applicative f where
   pure :: a -> f a
   (<*>) :: f (a -> b) -> f a -> f b
```

Example:

haskell

Copy code

```
pure (+) <*> Just 2 <*> Just 3 -- Result: Just 5
[(+1), (*2)] <*> [1, 2, 3] -- Result: [2,3,4,2,4,6]
```

3. Monads

Monad is another level of abstraction, extending Applicative with the ability to chain operations that depend on previous results.

Definition:

haskell

Copy code

```
class Applicative m => Monad m where
  (>>=) :: m a -> (a -> m b) -> m b
```

Example:

haskell

Copy code

```
Just 3 >>= (\x -> Just (x * 2)) -- Result: Just 6
```

4. Foldable and Traversable

Foldable: Abstracts over data structures that can be folded to a single value.

haskell

Copy code

```
foldr (+) 0 [1, 2, 3] -- Result: 6
```

Traversable: Allows traversing data structures while applying a function within a context.

haskell

Copy code

```
traverse Just [1, 2, 3] -- Result: Just [1, 2, 3]
```

5. Category and Arrow

Category: Generalizes the idea of composable functions.

haskell

Copy code

```
class Category cat where
  (.) :: cat b c -> cat a b -> cat a c
  id :: cat a a
```

Arrow: Extends Category to model computations that have inputs and outputs, like pipelines.

Why These Concepts Matter:

Code Reusability: Abstracts like Functor and
Applicative allow writing generic functions that work with many types.

Composability: These abstractions enable building complex operations by combining smaller ones.
Expressiveness: They provide tools to model and solve problems in a concise and elegant way.

By understanding and utilizing these abstractions, Haskell developers can write cleaner, more expressive, and highly reusable code.

Best Practices in Haskell Programming

Haskell's functional paradigm and strong type system offer unique advantages, but they also require a thoughtful approach to programming. Following best practices ensures code quality, maintainability, and performance.

1. Leverage the Type System

Haskell's type system is one of its greatest strengths. Use it to enforce invariants, document your intentions, and catch errors at compile time.

Use strongly-typed custom data types for clarity and safety.
Utilize type synonyms and newtype for better readability.
Prefer explicit type annotations to improve code clarity and help debugging.

2. Emphasize Purity

Write pure functions wherever possible. Pure functions are predictable, testable, and easier to reason about.

Avoid side effects in most of your codebase.
Use the IO monad or other effect-handling abstractions for side effects, isolating them from the core logic.

3. Modular Code Design

Break your program into small, reusable modules and functions.

Follow the single responsibility principle: each function should perform one well-defined task.
Use higher-order functions for abstraction and code reuse.

4. Adopt Idiomatic Haskell Practices

Write idiomatic Haskell by understanding and using common patterns.

Use list comprehensions for concise iteration.
Prefer function composition ((.)) over deeply nested function calls.
Take advantage of pattern matching for clear and expressive code.

5. Use Lazy Evaluation Wisely

While laziness is powerful, it can introduce performance pitfalls.

Avoid retaining large unevaluated thunks; use strict evaluation (seq, deepseq) when necessary.
Profile your code to detect and fix memory leaks.

6. Make Effective Use of Abstractions

Haskell offers many powerful abstractions like Functor, Applicative, and Monad.

Learn and use these abstractions appropriately to simplify complex logic.
Avoid over-abstraction, which can make the code harder to understand.

7. Write Readable and Maintainable Code

Prioritize readability for your future self and collaborators.

Write clear and descriptive variable and function names.
Add comments and documentation for complex or non-obvious code.
Follow Haskell's community standards, such as indentation and formatting conventions.

8. Test Thoroughly

Testing ensures code correctness and helps maintain stability.

Use QuickCheck for property-based testing to verify that your code behaves as expected under various inputs. Write unit tests for critical parts of your application.

9. Optimize Performance When Necessary

Focus on correctness first, then optimize.

Use profiling tools like GHC's profiler to identify bottlenecks.
Replace slow algorithms with more efficient alternatives, leveraging Haskell's libraries.
Utilize parallelism and concurrency features like par, pseq, and STM to improve performance on multicore systems.

10. Engage with the Haskell Ecosystem

Haskell has a rich ecosystem of libraries and tools.

Use Cabal or Stack for dependency management and building projects.
Explore libraries on Hackage for prebuilt solutions to common problems.
Stay updated with the community for new tools and techniques.

By adhering to these best practices, Haskell programmers can write clean, efficient, and maintainable code, fully leveraging the language's capabilities for functional programming.

Avoiding Common Pitfalls in Functional Programming

Functional programming (FP) offers many advantages, such as improved readability, testability, and composability. However, it also introduces unique challenges. Being aware of common pitfalls can help developers fully harness the power of FP while avoiding potential problems.

1. Misunderstanding Purity and Side Effects

Problem: Failing to isolate side effects can lead to impure code, undermining FP principles.
Solution: Keep functions pure by avoiding state mutation and external dependencies. Use monads like IO or State to manage side effects explicitly.

2. Overusing Recursion

Problem: Over-reliance on recursion can lead to stack overflows or inefficient solutions.
Solution: Use tail recursion or leverage built-in higher-order functions like map, fold, and filter, which are optimized for performance.

3. Neglecting Laziness

Problem: Lazy evaluation can create unexpected memory usage (thunks), leading to space leaks.
Solution: Profile the application to identify thunks and use strict evaluation (seq, deepseq) where appropriate. Be mindful of lazy data structures.

4. Ignoring Type System Benefits

Problem: Not leveraging Haskell's strong type system can lead to less robust and harder-to-maintain code.
Solution: Use types to encode invariants and constraints. Define custom data types and type aliases for clarity and safety.

5. Over-Abstraction

Problem: Excessive use of abstractions like monads, higher-order functions, or combinators can make code hard to understand.

Solution: Strike a balance between abstraction and simplicity. Avoid premature optimization and ensure abstractions are well-documented.

6. Improper Error Handling

Problem: Failing to handle errors explicitly can lead to runtime failures or uninformative messages.
Solution: Use monads like Maybe or Either for safe and explicit error handling. Combine them with pattern matching for clarity.

7. Insufficient Testing

Problem: Assuming that the type system will catch all errors without thorough testing can lead to bugs.
Solution: Complement the type system with property-based testing tools like QuickCheck and write unit tests for critical functions.

8. Neglecting Performance Considerations

Problem: Writing clean but inefficient functional code can lead to performance issues in real-world applications.
Solution: Profile and optimize performance-critical sections. Use efficient data structures like Vector and libraries designed for speed, such as bytestring or text.

9. Not Utilizing the Ecosystem

Problem: Reinventing the wheel by implementing functionality already available in libraries.
Solution: Explore existing libraries on platforms like Hackage and embrace community solutions for common problems.

10. Overlooking Concurrency and Parallelism

Problem: Not taking advantage of FP's strengths in writing concurrent and parallel code can limit scalability.

Solution: Use tools like Software Transactional Memory (STM), the async library, or parallel constructs for clean and efficient concurrent programming.

11. Poor Code Organization

Problem: Keeping all logic in one module or using cryptic names reduces readability.
Solution: Structure your code into well-defined modules, use meaningful names, and adhere to Haskell's style guide.

12. Inadequate Documentation

Problem: Functional code, especially with complex abstractions, can be hard to understand without proper documentation.
Solution: Write clear comments, explain your abstractions, and use tools like Haddock to generate documentation.

By being mindful of these pitfalls, developers can maximize the benefits of functional programming and produce robust, efficient, and maintainable applications.

www.ingramcontent.com/pod-product-compliance
Lightning Source LLC
LaVergne TN
LVHW022333060326
832902LV00022B/4009
* 9 7 9 8 3 0 1 6 4 7 0 5 5 *